Vienna

Philippe Bénet and
Renata Holzbachová

CITYSCAPE

JPMGUIDES

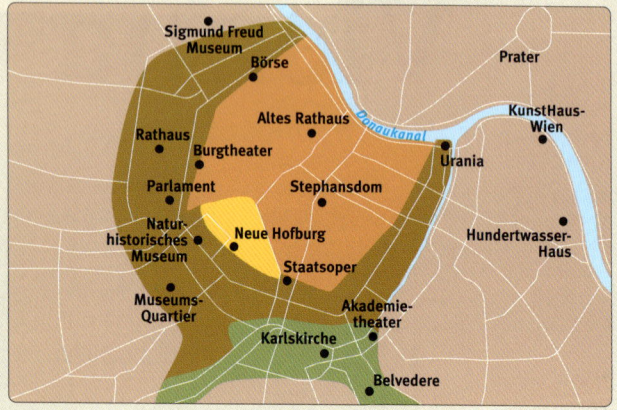

Many famous sights await discovery in Vienna's city centre, or *Innere Stadt*, enclosed by the Ring boulevard and easily reached on foot. Yet there's lots more to be seen elsewhere. We have divided the city into five large areas, to be explored at your own pace. We have included some interesting trips into the outskirts under the heading Excursions.

Contents

Features
Sissi: Myth and Reality 15
Music's World Capital 19
Vienna for Children 58
Psychoanalysis 70
A Taste of Vienna 80
Sachertorte 86
Writing in Vienna 96

Map
Around Vienna 108
Hofburg 110

Fold-out map
Vienna (Centre)
Local transport
(U- and S-Bahn)

cityLights	5
cityPast	9
citySights	21
City Centre	22
The Hofburg	36
The Ring	42
Karlsplatz and the Belvedere	50
Outer Districts	60
Excursions	74
cityBites	83
cityNights	91
cityFacts	101
Index	111

Symbols:
- ★ Our favourites
- **U** U-Bahn (subway)
- Ⓢ S-Bahn (rapid train)
- 🚋 Tram

cityLights

The Viennese pendulum swings forever back and forth between dream and reality. The name conjures up a vision of waltzes and operettas, of revolutionaries and artists imagining new worlds in cosy coffee-houses, of lovers hurrying away from a Schubert piano recital to sip new wine in a *Heuriger* wine garden.

This is all still true. But Vienna is also a town of hard-headed businessmen leading a thriving economy into the new Europe.

The bowler-hatted cabby who trots his horse-drawn Fiaker past the Hofburg imperial palace delights in telling endless romantic tales of the Vienna Woods, of the trysts and suicides of wayward Habsburg archdukes and their mistresses and other lovers. And the taxi-driver threading his Mercedes through the noonday traffic on the Ringstrasse takes equal pleasure in his cynical spin on the latest world crisis or another corruption scandal on the Vienna Stock Exchange. The town provides the obvious setting for one of its most illustrious sons, psychoanalyst Sigmund Freud, to have dissected the dreams that reveal the sombre side of man's and woman's unconscious. Darkness and light are everywhere.

Yes, the Viennese are charming. The effect is accentuated by the melodious flow of their language. But the charm may also be accompanied by an undercurrent of sometimes malicious irony, the notorious *Wiener Schmäh* (Viennese sarcasm), that can catch the visitor unawares. Just take it as the spice of life, like the *Kren* (horseradish sauce) that adds a sharp touch to the celebrated delicacy, *Tafelspitz*— boiled beef. Without this keen ironic edge, the distinctive atmosphere of *Gemütlichkeit,* the snug warmth that is the city's preferred mode of life, might be insufferably cloying.

At the Heart of Europe

A glance at names in the telephone book shows, besides the dominant community whose German language prevails, the varied origins of its citizens—Czech, Slovak, Polish, Hungarian, Italian, Turkish and representatives of all the states of former Yugoslavia. The town is full of descendants and more recent immigrants from the twelve nations whose 51 million inhabitants made up the Austro-Hungarian Empire until its break-up in 1918. Enriched by these various languages and cuisines, Austria has become a cultural melting pot, blending influences from practically all corners of Europe.

Cradle of Culture

In an Austrian population of some 8 million, Vienna numbers over 1.7 million. The city is both national capital and, as the *Land Wien*, one of the nine states (*Bundesländer*) of the Federal Republic of Austria. It is divided into 23 districts (*Bezirke*) covering a total surface of 415 sq km (160 sq miles). The town is surrounded by extensive forests and vineyards. The Danube crosses the northeastern suburbs, but only in our imagination, thanks to the waltz of Johann Strauss, is the river ever blue.

The city prides itself on its rich creative tradition—the streets "paved with culture, as the streets of other towns are paved with asphalt," declared writer Karl Kraus at the beginning of the 20th century. Streets and monuments alike, concert halls, Opera House and Burgtheater, the imperial palaces of Hofburg, Schönbrunn and Belvedere, are laden with the greatest names of Europe's musical, literary, artistic and architectural traditions: composers Brahms, Beethoven, Mozart, Haydn, Schubert and Strauss, more recently Mahler, Schönberg and Webern; writers Schnitzler,

Zweig, Musil and Thomas Bernhard; painters Klimt, Kokoschka and Schiele; architects Adolf Loos and Otto Wagner. And the city pays due tribute to Freud, quite as much great writer as pioneering scientist.

The Coffeehouse

The second Turkish siege of Vienna in 1683 had two happy consequences. The Ottoman armies were repelled, but they left behind the noble art of coffee making, which the Viennese turned into a whole way of life.

Business, pleasure and romance all begin or end in a Kaffeehaus. The choice for the appropriate place is endless. The bourgeoisie plumped for the delicacies of Demel, the imperial café and pastry shop, or its rival in the Sacher hotel. Painters have discussed their new works in the Hawelka. Writers made their second home in the Griensteidl, Alt-Wien, Prückel or Central.

Waiters work at a leisurely pace, so don't get impatient. Try a cake or fruit tart with whipped cream, or read one of a dozen international newspapers hung out for you on a central table. Get to know one of the many kinds of coffee, each served with a glass of cold water.

One, Two, Three, One…

Vienna has five seasons—spring, summer, autumn, winter, then the ball season. Grand balls are held throughout the *Fasching* (Carnival) from November 11 to Ash Wednesday. The haunting music of Johann Strauss conjures up images of Franz Joseph opening the dance with his Empress Sissi. Today the Ball still has its formal place in Vienna's winter programme. Ladies put on a long dress, gentleman don white tie and tails or at least a dinner jacket. And the dance goes on till 5am, when the coffeehouses provide an appropriate *Katerfrühstück* (literally "hangover breakfast").

Sons and daughters of the Old Vienna aristocracy still learn their steps at dance schools, preparing them for the waltz and foxtrot at one of the more prestigious events like the *Juristenball*, the Lawyers' Ball. Equally appreciated are those of the pastry-chefs, the hunters or the policemen. The most glorious, however, is the Opera Ball. Every year, on the Thursday before Shrove Tuesday, 7,000 crème de la crème gather to dance, to see and be seen. Young ladies all in white venture onto the gleaming parquet floor of the State Opera. The Master of Ceremonies formally opens the ball with the words *"Alles Waltzer"*—"Waltz, everybody!"

cityPast

The Vienna region has been inhabited since prehistoric times and was always coveted because of its geographical position. Celts lived here in the 4th century BC and were driven out by the Romans some 300 years later.

The outpost of Vindobona (Celtic: "White Field") which developed into Vienna took on great significance because neighbours to the north were interested in using the Danube as an important trade route. Emperor Marcus Aurelius died here in AD 180. As the power of the Roman Empire declined, Vienna was frequently invaded by barbarians and finally destroyed around AD 400. It was subsequently occupied by a Germanic tribe from Bavaria.

Towards the end of the 8th century, Charlemagne incorporated the Ostmark (East March) with Vienna into his European empire. Within a hundred years, the Magyars had conquered the region from Hungary.

Retrieved by the Babenberg dynasty, the lands were inherited by the newly created Holy Roman Empire in 976. The name Austria *(Ostarrichi)* first appeared in 996 in a document signed by Emperor Otto III.

Birth of Austria

Over the next three centuries, the empire expanded under the Babenbergs. In 1156, Emperor Frederick I made the East Mark a duchy with Vienna as its capital. Henry II moved his court from the Leopoldsberg, a nearby hill overlooking the Danube, to what was to become the Hofburg palace.

The town grew in beauty. A new city wall was built with the ransom money paid for King Richard the Lionheart. The Austrians had captured him in 1192 on his way home from the Third Crusade. Vienna soon became a centre of trade and culture, with a population of over 10,000.

After a victory over the Hungarians in 1246, Emperor Frederick II fell from his horse and with him went the Babenberg dynasty. Austria passed to Bohemia, and the Holy Roman Empire stayed without an emperor from 1254 to 1273. Finally, Rudolf I von Habsburg was elected German king, and the House of Habsburg ruled Austria till the end of World War I.

The Habsburgs

Rudolf asked Ottokar II of Bohemia to hand back Austria. After the Bohemian king's death in the battle of Marchfeld in August 1278, one of the largest knight battles of the Middle ages, Austria returned to the Holy Roman (German) Empire. Four years later, Rudolf I gave his sons Albrecht and Rudolf the fiefdoms of Austria and Styria (Steiermark).

The Habsburgs wanted to elevate Vienna to the ecclesiastic rank of bishopric. In the early 14th century they began to build St Stephan's cathedral in place of the Romanesque church consecrated in 1147. In 1365, Duke Rudolf IV founded the University of Vienna, second oldest university in the German-speaking world, after Prague (1348).

Duke Albrecht V von Habsburg became king of Hungary in 1437 and king of Bohemia a year later. With the name Albrecht II, he made Vienna the capital of the Holy Roman (German) Empire.

After the death of his brother Albrecht, Frederick III was the last German emperor who had himself crowned in Rome. The crown was now hereditary and Austria was elevated in 1453 to rank of archduchy. During civil-insurrection in 1462, the Viennese citizenry besieged the Hofburg for two months, with the emperor and his family barricaded inside.

Inaugurating Austria's matrimonial policy, which reached its climax under Charles V, Frederick III arranged the marriage of his son Maximilian I to Mary of Burgundy, who brought as her dowry the earldom of Burgundy and the Netherlands. Matthias Corvinus, King of Hungary, coined the phrase: *"Bella gerant alii, tu felix Austria nubes"* ("Let others wage war, you, happy Austria, get married.")

Maximilian I, King of Rome and German Emperor, set about reorganizing his empire. After declaring what are now Austrian federal states to be "hereditary lands", he was obliged to make compromises with the German princes who refused centralization. Thus were created, among other things, the supreme court and the chancellory.

In 1515, Maximilian I celebrated in St Stephan's cathedral the double wedding of his grandson Ferdinand and granddaughter Mary with the children of Ladislas II, king of Hungary and Bohemia. Consequently these lands became part of the Habsburg empire.

After his death, his grandson Charles V, who already owned Castile, Aragon, the Netherlands, parts of Latin America, Naples, Sicily and Spain's overseas possessions, became German ruler. He reigned from 1519 to 1556 over an empire on which the sun never set.

The ideas of the Renaissance gained ground throughout the continent and the Reformation spread through Germany, much to the displeasure of the emperor.

Turkish Sieges

Soon another danger threatened the empire. Sultan Suleiman the Magnificent occupied Hungary and laid siege to Vienna with an army of 120,000 in September 1529. Count Niklas Salm's garrison of 20,000 soldiers resisted the attacks and forced the Turks to retreat. Nonetheless, the danger of a Turkish invasion remained for another 150 years.

After the abdication of Charles V, his brother Ferdinand I, already heir to the thrones of Bohemia and Hungary, became ruler of Austria in 1556.

Eight years later, he was succeeded by his son Maximilian II. Although he supported the Catholic Counter-Reformation of the Jesuits, he also called for tolerance and promoted the Reformation movement. Under his rule, some 80 per cent of the population converted to the Protestant faith. Ruling from 1576, his son Rudolf II guaranteed the Protestants freedom of worship.

At the beginning of the 17th century, however, the Counter-Reformation triumphed. In the Thirty Years' War (1618–48), the town was threatened by the Bohemian army in 1619 and the Swedish army in 1645. Three years later, the Peace of Westphalia put an end to the confusion.

Vienna had scarcely recovered from the plague of 1679 when the Turks returned to besiege the city. In 1683, Grand Vizir Kara Mustapha massed a force of 200,000 men at the city gates. The 15,000 troops of Count Rüdiger von Starhemberg

Triumphal columns flank the Karlskirche, built to thank God for an answered prayer.

were powerless to stop the destruction of the city outskirts. It was only the heroic intervention of Prince Eugène of Savoy that finally forced the Ottoman armies to withdraw. For his loyal services he was rewarded with the two Belvedere palaces and a winter residence in the Himmelpfortgasse.

With the Turkish menace out of the way, Vienna started an intensive programme of construction, which gave the town much of its baroque character. Aristocrats of the Schwarzenberg, Kinzky, Lobkowitz and Lichtenstein families built splendid mansions around the city centre. At the same time, new buildings for the Hofburg, court library, Spanish Riding School and imperial chancellory were added. The jewel of Viennese baroque was the grand Karlskirche built for Emperor Charles IV by Johann and Joseph Fischer von Erlach. Under Empress Maria Theresa (1740–1780) the Habsburgs completed their summer residence, the opulent Schloss Schönbrunn.

Maria Theresa

Karl VI, who had no son, secured his succession by what the European royal courts acknowledged as the Pragmatic Sanction. His daughter Maria Theresa took over the government in return for her husband François renouncing his duchy of Lorraine. Nonetheless, after the death of Karl VI in 1740, the empress had to defend Habsburg possessions during an Austrian war of Succession that lasted eight years. The Treaty of Aachen confirmed in 1748 the Pragmatic Sanction and Maria Theresa could at last concern herself with legislative and administrative reforms and diplomacy. She bore 16 children, among them her heir Joseph II, and Marie Antoinette who met an unhappy end in the French Revolution.

Vienna became the capital of European music; its most famous composers included Joseph Haydn, Ludwig van Beethoven, Johann Strauss II and Wolfgang Amadeus Mozart.

Joseph II was crowned emperor after the death of his father in 1765, but had to share power with his mother. As an enlightened ruler he wanted to transform his empire into a modern state: he opened up to the whole population the hunting grounds of the Prater and Augarten, hitherto reserved for the aristocracy, fought privileges, introduced civil marriage and promulgated an edict of religious tolerance. At the death of Joseph II, Austria was weakened, but less because of these reforms than through the resistance they provoked.

Napoleon in Vienna

In 1792, war broke out between Revolutionary France and Austria. Franz II was the last Holy Roman (German) Emperor (1792–1806) and at the same time the first hereditary emperor of Austria under the name Franz I (1804–35).

In 1805, Napoleon launched a new offensive on Austria and occupied Vienna. The following year, Franz I renounced his crown, and the Holy Roman Empire was dissolved. Vienna revolted in 1809, and Napoleon was defeated at Essling but was victorious two months later at Wagram. During his second occupation, the French emperor had the city shelled for 24 hours on end. Many paintings from the imperial gallery in the Belvedere were carried off to France. The composer Haydn, old and feeble, died of grief, even though Napoleon had him tended by his personal bodyguard.

Napoleon lived out at Schönbrunn and visited the town only at night, by torchlight. His marriage to Maria Luise, daughter of Franz I, took place in the Augustinerkirche in 1810. She bore him a son, the Duke of Reichstadt and King of Rome, who died of tuberculosis at 21.

After Napoleon's abdication, the Congress of Vienna assembled numerous princes and statesmen who worked out a new order for Europe under the influence of the arch-conservative Austrian chancellor, Prince Metternich—between dances at the Hofburg palace.

The subsequent quiet years of the stolid Biedermeier period proved a glorious era for music: Beethoven and Schubert created immortal works, Johann Strauss father and son conquered the world with their melodies. But political oppression and police dictatorship led to the revolution of 1848. From March to October, insurrection grew, culminating in the assassination of the war minister. Chancellor Metternich fled Vienna. Ferdinand I, son of Franz I, was forced to abdicate and was succeeded by his 18-year-old nephew, Franz Joseph.

Franz Joseph and Sissi

While the empress felt very close to the Hungarian people, Franz Joseph was much beloved among the Viennese. Under his long reign (1848–1919), the capital took on its present-day appearance. From 1857, fortifications were removed and replaced by the broad boulevard of the Ringstrasse, with imposing buildings like the Parliament, City Hall and Univer-

SISSI: MYTH AND REALITY

In the 1950s, the cinema drew a picture of Sissi (Sisi in German) that was kitschy and divorced from all reality. Empress Elisabeth (1837–98) was an intelligent and cultivated woman who worried little about court etiquette and much about the destiny of the Hungarian people. She spent a long time in the vicinity of Budapest. The sensitive empress was very much concerned about her physical appearance. For this she imposed iron discipline with exercise and a constant diet. From her 30th birthday, she refused to let herself be photographed.

After her marriage with her cousin Franz Joseph at the age of 16, she had to exchange a hitherto fairly free life in Bavaria for the strict supervision of her mother-in-law, Sophie, who also later took over the education of the children. The empress fell ill and took refuge in the milder climate of Madeira—the first of a long series of journeys abroad.

In June 1867, her efforts for more recognition for the Hungarian people reaped their reward. The imperial couple were crowned King and Queen of Hungary: the dual monarchy was born. Even this, however, did not keep Sissi in the palace. After she had given her husband four children, she decided at 40 to distance herself still further from court and pursue her passion for poetry and travel.

The empress never fully recovered from the suicide of her only son, Crown Prince Rudolf, in January 1889. The heir to the throne first murdered his 17 year old mistress, Baroness Maria von Vetsera, then took his own life, whilst on the royal hunting estate of Mayerling. Nine years later, on holiday in Geneva and out walking on the Quai du Mont-Blanc, Elisabeth was stabbed to death by the Italian anarchist Luigi Lucheni.

sity. Vienna's cultural life took on a new lease of life. The Staatsoper (State Opera) opened in 1869, the Volksoper (People's Opera) in 1898; followed by the Musikverein and other concert halls. From 1891, the famous art and science museums were opened to the public. Spacious parks brought the town more greenery, and the city was modernized with a tramway, the Urania planetarium and the Prater's giant ferris wheel.

But Franz Joseph's reign was also marked by personal tragedy: his unhappy marriage to the lovely Sissi; the tragic death of his brother Maximilian, who was shot by revolutionaries in Mexico in 1867; the suicide of his son and heir Rudolf, with his mistress, in 1889; the murder of his wife by an Italian anarchist in 1898 in Geneva, and finally the assassination in 1914 of his nephew Archduke Franz Ferdinand in Sarajevo, which led to World War I.

At the same time, several crises beset the Austro-Hungarian Empire and hastened its dissolution. The dual monarchy guaranteed Hungary more independence in 1867; only the foreign, finance and war ministries were shared with Austria. Despite his will to hold the empire together, Franz Joseph was confronted with the demands of several national minorities. Participation in the alliance system of the German Chancellor Bismarck enabled him to continue on an international level until the end of the 19th century, but Franz Joseph's efforts to dominate the Balkans finally led to the collapse of the Austro-Hungarian monarchy.

End of the Empire

Vienna numbered 2 million inhabitants in 1910. After the assassination of Archduke Franz Ferdinand, Austria's policy of alliances drove the land headlong into World War I. In the capital, there were severe shortages as food was rationed due to Hungary refusing to support the war effort. Currency devaluation ruined the propertied classes and living conditions deteriorated throughout the country.

Franz Joseph died in 1916, aged 86. His grandnephew Karl I succeeded him and was forced to abdicate and leave Austria in November, 1918. The last emperor of Austria-Hungary died of pneumonia, aged 34, four years later whilst in exile on the island of Madeira. A republic was proclaimed. In 1919, the Saint-Germain and Trianon treaties sealed the fate the dual monarchy and prohibited annexation *(Anschluss)* to Germany.

Red Vienna
The disproportionately large capital of the shrunken state of Austria came under the influence of the Social Democrats, who remained in power till February 1934. The "red" government effected considerable achievements in the areas of health and social welfare. A new style of social housing created new neighbourhoods on the city outskirts. However, tensions grew between the bourgeoisie and the government. A workers' demonstration in July 1927 ended with the burning of the central courthouse and bloody street-battles. The consequences of the worldwide economic crisis exacerbated radical tendencies and led in 1934 to civil war between democrats and fascists. Chancellor Engelbert Dollfuss enacted an authoritarian Christian constitution. During an abortive Nazi Putsch, the chancellor was assassinated in July 1934. His successor Kurt von Schuschnigg clung with difficulty to power until he was forced by Hitler to resign in March 1938.

Anschluss (Annexation)
After the German invasion in March 1938, Austria became part of the Nazis' Third Reich, with the enthusiastic support of a large part of the Austrian population. Viennese citizens—Social Democrats, Communists and Jews—were among the first to be deported to the concentration camps of Dachau (in Bavaria) and Mauthausen (on the Danube east of Linz). Many others joined the SS and became active members of the Nazi Party. Between 1938 and 1945, some 6,000 citizens were executed in Vienna's city prison, thousands of others were persecuted for religious, political or "racial" reasons. From 1943, Allied bombardment inflicted considerable damage. In the last six months of the war, more than 50 air raids caused 12,000 deaths and destroyed large areas of the city, leaving an estimated 270,000 homeless. All Danube bridges were blown up, with the exception of the Reichsbrücke. Almost all museums and architectural monuments were damaged, including St Stephan's Cathedral and the Opera House.

The Second Republic
In April 1945, the town was liberated by the Soviet Army and then divided up by the Allies into American, British, French and Soviet zones. During the 10 years of the military occupation, Vienna was a meeting place for spies and smugglers.

On May 15, 1955, the Austrian State Treaty gave the country its independence, along with an obligatory declaration of neutrality. The new status was celebrated with great festivities. The Opera House, Burgtheater and Spanish Riding School were ceremoniously re-opened.

Socialist chancellor Bruno Kreisky (1970–83) gave the city a new élan. Due to its geographical situation and neutrality, Vienna became the seat of several international organizations like OPEC (Organization of Petroleum Exporting Countries), the International Atomic Energy Agency and various organs of the United Nations.

In 1986, former United Nations Secretary General Kurt Waldheim was elected President of Austria, despite his wartime involvement with Nazi Germany. In recent years, the perennial government coalition of the socialist SPÖ and conservative ÖVP *(Volkspartei)* has been threatened by the ever-growing extreme rightwing party FPÖ *(Freiheiheitliche Partei)*.

In January 1995, Austria became a full member of the European Union, and the Euro was introduced in 2002. In 2006 Vienna and Salzburg celebrated the 250th birthday of Mozart.

The new Donau City commercial, residential and leisure district has re-shaped the Viennese skyline.

MUSIC'S WORLD CAPITAL

Vienna's climb to its position as virtually undisputed world capital of music began in the Middle Ages. It was around 1200 that Walther von der Vogelweide, the most important lyricist in the German-speaking world, learned his art at the court of the Babenberg dynasty in Vienna. Austrian music would always derive its distinctively seductive elegance from the dual influences of Mediterranean and Germanic culture. While in the 17th century the city on the Danube drew almost all its inspiration from the Italian composers, it soon experienced a first flowering of its musical magic in the age of the Baroque. In the 18th century, first the powerful operatic acheivements of Gluck, then the emergence of Haydn and Mozart gave Vienna the definitive status of musical capital. The latter two composers together with Beethoven ushered in the period that came to be known as Wiener Klassik (Viennese Classicism).

The town's musical heyday extended from the last third of the 18th century to the first half of the 20th. In this period, an impressive list of great talents added their names to Vienna's fame: Schubert, Bruckner, Brahms, Wolf, Mahler, Schönberg and Webern. Princes fought to exchange their patronage for the privilege of having some of the compowers' works dedicated to them.

Vienna's very own genre of operettas and waltzes carried the city to a new pinnacle, led by Lehár and Strauss, father and son. In the early 20th century, the 12-tone music of the second Vienna School of Schönberg and Webern gave rise to a musical revoution. Still attracting the world's greatest singers and conductors, the Vienna Opera and Vienna Philharmonic Orchestra remain revered ambassadors for the city's music—not least of all with the orchestra's annual New Year's Concert, televised in over 50 countries.

citySights

City Centre	22
Vienna's historic core, around Stephansdom	
The Hofburg	36
Heart of the Empire and the Habsburgs' centre of power	
The Ring	42
Emperor Franz Joseph's Ceremonial Way	
Karlsplatz and the Belvedere	50
From baroque Karlskirche to the elegant Schloss Belvedere	
Outer Districts	60
Schloss Schönbrunn and some unusual museums	
Excursions	74
Kahlenberg, Vienna Woods and Wachau	

CITY CENTRE

Vienna's landmark, St Stephen's Cathedral (Stephansdom), rises from the heart of the historic 1st district that is encircled by the boulevard called the Ringstrasse. From the cathedral square, Stephansplatz, you can reach most of the sights in this chapter on foot (U-Bahn stations Stephansplatz or Herrengasse).

THE DISTRICT AT A GLANCE

🏛 SIGHTS

Architecture
Stephansdom ★ 22
Haas-Haus 24
Graben 24
Loos-Haus 26
Bundeskanzleramt ... 26
Palais Collalto 28
Wipplingerstrasse 29
Bäckerstrasse 30
Winterpalais des Prinzen Eugen 31
Singerstrasse 31
Annagasse 32

Atmosphere
Kohlmarkt ★ 25
Fleischmarkt 31

Browsing
Demel ★ 25
Herrengasse 26
Kärntner Strasse ★ ... 32

Churches
Peterskirche 25
Michaelerkirche 26
Schottenstift 28
Zu den neun Chören der Engel 28
Maria am Gestade 29
Ruprechtskirche 29
Kapuzinerkirche 33

Museums
Jüdisches Museum ... 26
Feuerwehrmuseum .. 28
Uhrenmuseum 28
Mozarthaus Vienna .. 31

Haus der Musik ★ 32
Österreichisches Theatermuseum 33

Remembrance
Rauhensteingasse 32
Kaisergruft 33

Squares
Freyung ★ 27
Am Hof 28
Judenplatz 29
Hoher Markt ★ 30
Franziskanerplatz 31
Neuer Markt 33

🚶 **WALKING TOUR** 34

☕ **WINING AND DINING** 84

Stephansdom (E4) The city's landmark is known affectionately as the Steffl. It took over 250 years to build and combines several different styles. In their effort to elevate Vienna to a bishopric in the 14th century, the Habsburgs added a monumental Gothic choir to the late-Romanesque basilica dating from the Babenberg era. The original church was later destroyed but retained its west

A friendly cab driver waiting to take you for a ride.

façade—the Heiden towers and Riesentor (Giants' Door)—which Rudolf IV completed with two Gothic chapels. The steeple and central nave were added in the 15th century. At the beginning of the 16th century, a second tower was planned for the north side, but the threat of Turkish attack diverted the money to expanding the city's fortifications. The unfinished Eagle Tower (Adlerturm) was given a Renaissance roof in 1578. It houses the 20-ton Pummerin bell, cast from the brass of 100 captured Turkish cannons.

The Stephansdom is Austria's largest Gothic building. The south tower, 137 m (463 ft) high, and the roof covered with 230,000 coloured tiles are visible from afar. The roof is adorned with the two-headed eagle and imperial crown, and the Order of the Golden Fleece, emblem of the Habsburgs.

Accessible through the Riesentor in the west façade, the main entrance is flanked by two Gothic chapels. In the Tirna Chapel (left) is the tomb of Prince Eugène. The right chapel is dedicated to St Alois. The impressive nave is about 170 m (560 ft) long and 39 m (128 ft) wide. Note the superb rib vaulting borne aloft on mighty pillars. A masterpiece of Gothic sculpture dominates the nave: the pulpit carved in 1500 by Anton Pilgram of Brno. It is decorated with rosettes, stalactites and finely sculpted leaves. Salamanders and toads symbolize good and evil. The artist has immortalized himself peeping through a window. Another self-portrait of Pilgram (with square and compass) decorates the foot of the organ. The exquisite Servants' Madonna *(Dienstbotenmadonna)* leaning on a pillar in front of the main altar dates from the year 1340. On the south side of the choir, the sarcophagus of Friedrich III is a shining example of Dutch art. The splendid Wiener Neustadter Altar in the left transept was created in 1447. The catacombs (entrance in the north tower, daily tours) are gloomy but quite interesting, particularly the dukes' tombs of the Habsburgs.

Outside in the pavement on the south side of Stephansplatz, a geometric pattern in red tiles traces the floor plan of the Magdalene Chapel, burned down in 1781. The square directly at the corner of Graben and Kärntner Strasse is known as Stock im Eisen (Stump in Iron). The name refers to a tree-stump into which journeymen locksmiths drove in a nail at the beginning of their apprenticeship when they left Vienna. • Mon–Sat 6am–10pm; Sun, holidays 7am–10pm. Guided tours Mon–Sat 10.30am–3pm; Sun, holidays 3pm. Evening tour including roof June–Sept Sat 7pm. South Tower: daily 9am–5.30pm. Pummerin bell Apr–Oct 8.30am–5.30pm; July, Aug 8.30am–6pm; Nov–Mar to 5pm. Guided tours in English Apr–Oct daily 3.45pm; Jun–Sept Sat at 5.30pm ☎515 52-3526 • Ⓤ 1, 3: Stephansplatz

Haas-Haus (E4) The Steffl is reflected in the modern glass façade of the Haas-Haus (1985–90), at first a controversial building but which has now made itself at home. Besides its fashionable and expensive boutiques, a first-class restaurant here affords a magnificent view of the city. Ⓤ 1, 3: Stephansplatz

Around the Graben (D4) The fortification moat *(Graben)* from the Roman era was filled in during the 13th century. It served as a vegetable market in the Middle Ages and became famous in the 18th century for the favours of its so-called Graben Nymphs. Today the long space is one of the most elegant squares in Vienna, with expensive shops and open-air café terraces. In the middle stands the baroque Pestsäule (Plague Pillar) erected by Leopold I in memory of the 1679 epidemic which cost some 100,000 lives. Adolf Loos's Jugendstil (Art

Nouveau) facilities in the middle of the Graben demonstrate that even public toilets can have artistic value. Among the noteworthy monuments are the baroque Palais Bartolotti-Partenfeld (no. 11), the neoclassical Spar-Casse (Savings Bank) building (21) and the Haus zur grünen Wiese (Green Meadows, 8) built for the pastry chefs' guild in 1705, with a décor of old-fashioned cake tins. The Anker House (10) is the work of Jugendstil architect Otto Wagner. Playwright Bertolt Brecht and satirist Walter Mehring met in the Café de l'Europe (31) in the 1930s; it was modernized in the 1950s. 🅄 1,3: Stephansplatz

Peterskirche (D3) Turning right off the Graben, Jungferngasse leads over to the slender Peterskirche, whose dome was inspired by that of St Peter's in Rome. The church was begun by Italian architect Gabriele Montani in 1702 and completed by baroque master Johann Lukas von Hildebrandt, with two towers rising at an angle to the main structure. The interior decoration is opulent. The painting in the ceiling of the dome depicts the Assumption. On the left, note Matthias Steinl's baroque pulpit and Lorenzo Mattielli's altar dedicated to St John of Nepomuk. A loggia features the two-headed eagle of the Habsburgs.
• Mon–Fri 7am–7pm; Sat, Sun and holidays from 9am. Free organ recitals Mon–Fri at 3pm, Sat, Sun at 8pm • Petersplatz 🅄 1, 3: Stephansplatz

Kohlmarkt (D4) Vienna's "Bond Street" leads from the Graben to the emperor's winter residence. Charcoal for fuel was sold here until the Hofburg was built in the 14th century, immediately upgrading the tone of the neighbourhood. Many of the shopfronts were designed by leading names of 20th-century architecture, such as Adolf Loos (Manz bookshop), Max Fabiani (Artariahaus) and Hans Hollein (nos. 7 and 8–10). Among the designer boutiques are the beautifully decorated windows of the famous pastry shop **Demel**, supplier of daintily packaged delicacies to the imperial family since 1789.

Michaelerkirche (D4) Across Michaelerplatz, at the intersection of Kohlmarkt and Herrengasse, you can see the entrance to the Hofburg. This site was already an important crossroads in ancient times. The church on the square was originally Romanesque, as can be seen from the nave and side aisles. The choir and belfry are both Gothic, while the façade is neoclassical. The finely carved portal, dating from the 18th century, depicts the Fall of the Angels. Michaelerkirche served as the imperial parish church, and some members of the Habsburg family are buried in the crypt. A funeral mass was said here in 1791 for Wolfgang Amadeus Mozart. • Daily 7am–10pm • Michaelerplatz 🆄 3: Herrengasse

Jüdisches Museum (D4) The museum is set in the 18th-century baroque Palais Eskeles, the former home of a Jewish banking family. It recounts the glory and horrors of Jewish life in Vienna through the ages (though the medieval period is covered by an annexe to the museum, the Misrachi Haus on Judenplatz). There's also a café, and a bookshop. • Sun–Fri 10am–6pm; closed Sat, Jewish New Year and Day of Atonement. Free guided tours Sun at 3pm (temporary exhibitions); 4pm (permanent collections) ☏535 04 31 • Dorotheergasse 11 🆄 3: Herrengasse

Loos-Haus (D4) This masterpiece of sober functional architecture designed by Adolf Loos (1870–1933) caused great controversy when it was built in 1911. The plain dark green façade was a disappointment to the Viennese, who were more accustomed to elaborate ornament. Emperor Franz Joseph protested by keeping his curtains drawn for weeks, to avoid seeing it. • Michaelerplatz 3 🆄 3: Herrengasse

Bundeskanzleramt (D4) The west wing of the Hofburg houses the Federal Chancellor's office and the Foreign Ministry. The Congress of Vienna held its conferences here from September 1814 to June 1815, and it was here that the Nazis assassinated Chancellor Dollfuss in 1934. • Ballhausplatz 2 🆄 3: Herrengasse

Herrengasse (D3–4) This has long been a prestigious address for the Viennese aristocracy. Among the palatial residences, look for the early 18th-century Palais Wilczek (no. 5); Palais Modena (7), now the Ministry of the Interior;

Frescoed ceiling by Carlo Carlone over the Grand Staircase in the Palais Daun-Kinsky.

Palais Mollard-Clary (9), housing a renowned Austrian art gallery; Palais Liechtenstein (13), built in the 16th century and renovated in the 19th. The Palais Ferstel, with its elegant entrance, was once the home of the Stock Exchange (now on the Schottenring). Inside, the building is a maze of courtyards and stairways. Beneath its arcades is the famous coffeehouse, the Café Central. 🆄 **3: Herrengasse**

Freyung (D3) This three-cornered square was once a gathering place for foreigners and thieves seeking refuge in the Schottenstift, a Benedictine mission. Two imposing mansions stand on the square—Hildebrandt's Palais Daun-Kinsky (1716) and the 17th-century Palais Harrach. Temporary exhibitions of works by modern and avant-garde artists are held in the **BA-CA Kunstforum**. In the middle of the Freyung, the Austria Fountain is embellished with allegorical figures representing the four most important rivers of the Habsburg Empire: Danube, Elbe, Weichsel and Po. 🆄 **3: Herrengasse**

Schottenstift (D2–3) The Scottish Mission and Scottish Church were founded by Irish Benedictine monks from the Scottish island of Iona in the 12th century. The church is known for two 17th-century altars and a monumental tomb by Fischer von Erlach, and the 13th-century statue of the Virgin is believed to have miraculous powers. Part of the same complex is a renowned high school, the Schottengymnasium, and a gallery of 15th–19th-century paintings. • Museum: Thurs–Sat 11am–5pm • Freyung 6 ☎534 98 600 **U** 3: Herrengasse

Am Hof (D3) The largest square of the Inner City was the site of the Babenberg dynasty's great castle, of which all trace has disappeared. Roman remains were discovered during reconstruction after World War II. Nowadays, an antique and art fair is held here at Easter and before Christmas. In the centre of the square stands the **Mariensäule** (Marian Column); its angels represent the struggle against the four scourges of humanity: famine (the dragon); war (the lion); plague (mythological basilisk with its lethal stare) and heresy (the serpent). **U** 1, 3: Stephansplatz or 3: Herrengasse

Zu den neun Choren der Engel (D3) Franz II proclaimed the end of the Holy Roman Empire from the balcony of the Nine Choirs of Angels church in 1806. Among the church's treasures are the organ, the high altar and the vault of the St Ignatius Chapel. • Am Hof

Palais Collalto (D3) Next to the Nine Choirs church, this baroque mansion is one of the city's many "Mozart addresses". It was here that the child prodigy gave his first public concert, at the age of 6. • Am Hof 13

Feuerwehrmuseum (D3) A superb collection of vintage fire engines, uniforms and fire-fighting apparatus relate the history of Vienna's fire brigade from 1686 to the present day. The old arsenal at No. 10 is now the palatial home of the fire brigade, topped by sculptures by Lorenzo Mattielli to the glory of the firemen. • Closed for renovation till mid 2009. ☎531 99 51 444 • Am Hof 7

Uhrenmuseum (D3) On a square behind the Nine Choirs church, the elegant Palais Obizzi (also called the Harfenhaus) houses Vienna's beautiful clock museum. The collection traces the technical and esthetic development of clocks and watches. • Tues–Sun (and holidays) 10am–6pm; free admission Sun ☎533 22 65 • Schulhof 2 **U** 1, 3: Stephansplatz or 3: Herrengasse

Judenplatz (D3) In the Middle Ages, this square was the centre of the Jewish quarter. Little remains of it today apart from the vestiges of a medieval synagogue, which you can see at the **Misrachi Haus** (no. 8), a multi-media museum documenting the life and circumstances of Viennese Jews in the Middle Ages (for opening times and telephone see the Jüdisches Museum, p. 26). At the 15th-century Haus zum Grossen Jordan, a Gothic relief depicts the baptism of Jesus, and an inscription in Latin recalls the destruction of the Jewish quarter in 1421, when 200 Jews were burned to death—"atoning for the terrible crimes of the Hebrew dogs". This is countered by a lesson in tolerance in the form of a statue of the great German humanist, philosopher and poet Gotthold Ephraim Lessing. The pale concrete **Holocaust Memorial**, by the British artist Rachel Whiteread, represents an inside-out library, the books with their spines towards the wall. The base is inscribed with the names of the death camps, and a dedication to the 65,000 Jewish Austrian dead. **U** 3: Herrengasse

Wipplingerstrasse (D2–3) This long thoroughfare is graced by two grand baroque buildings: the Bohemian High Chancellory, designed by Fischer von Erlach; and opposite, the Altes Rathaus (Old City Hall), which houses the archives of the Austrian anti-Nazi resistance movement. In the courtyard, an ornate 18th-century fountain by Georg Raphael Donner depicts Perseus saving the beautiful Andromeda from a sea-serpent. **U** 3: Herrengasse

Maria am Gestade (D–E2) Until its course was diverted, the Danube flowed past this slender church (St Mary on the Strand) with its filigree tower, used by the Danube sailors. The church was roughly contemporary with the Stephansdom and is a major achievement of Gothic architecture. Sculpted reliefs of John the Baptist and the Apostle John decorate the porch. Inside, see the 14th-century stained-glass windows and the fine Gothic-era paintings portraying the Annunciation and Coronation of the Virgin. **U** 3: Herrengasse

Ruprechtskirche (E3) On a height, this is the oldest church in Vienna. It is dedicated to St Rupert, the patron saint of Bavaria (650–718), whose statue

A QUICK COFFEE?

Not likely. In Vienna a coffee is to be savoured slowly. The choice is confusingly large.
Brauner: black with a dash of milk.
Einspänner: black with whipped cream, served in a tall glass.
Eiskaffee: black with whipped cream and vanilla ice cream.
Kapuziner: cappuccino.
Melange: frothy and milky, maybe with a blob of whipped cream.
Mocca: strong and black espresso.
Türkischer: boiling hot and sweet.

stands near the entrance. A chapel stood here in the 8th century; 400 years later a Romanesque church was built on its foundations. After reconstruction in the 13th and 15th centuries, only the nave and part of the tower remain from the Romanesque era.
• Easter to Christmas, Mon–Fri 10am–noon; Mon, Wed and Fri also 3–5pm; other times by appointment. Late night church Fri 9pm–midnight ☎ 535 60 03 • Seitenstettengasse 5/4 Ⓤ 1, 4: Schwedenplatz

Hoher Markt (E3) This square, the city's oldest, is the historic core of Vienna. Remains of the Roman Forum are visible inside the house at No. 3. The city market was held on the square in the Middle Ages, as well as public executions. The gallows were replaced in 1729 by the bronze and marble Vermählungsbrunnen, the fountain of the Wedding of the Virgin. Take a look, too, at the Jugendsti Anker Clock (set up by the Anker Insurance Co.), which has been going through its mechanical paces since 1914. On the hour, silhouettes of Marcus Aurelius, Maria Theresa, minstrel singer Walter von der Vogelweide, composer Joseph Haydn and various other historical figures make fleeting appearances. At noon, all 12 characters sally forth, with musical accompaniment. Ⓤ 1, 3: Stephansplatz

Bäckerstrasse (E3–4) The Schwanfeld House at No. 7 is worth a look for its splendid Renaissance courtyard and charming arcades. It was the home of 19th-century Biedermeier painter Friedrich Amerling. Opposite, Palais Seilern (8) was the Vienna home of French writer Madame de Staël. Notice on the façade of No. 12 (corner of Essiggasse) a charming little painting of a bespectacled cow and a wolf playing backgammon. Bars and cafés on this street are favourite night-time haunts for Vienna's artists. 🚇 1, 3: Stephansplatz

Fleischmarkt (E–F3) Schönlaterngasse leads to the old meat market. The butchers were eventually replaced by the Greek community. Apart from the Greek Orthodox church, the neighbourhood is famous for the restaurant known simply as the Griechenbeisl, which numbered among its guests Mozart, Strauss and Schubert, as well as writers Grillparzer and Nestroy. Further up the Fleischmarkt is the "Bermuda Triangle" of restaurants and bars, where Vienna's young crowd whiles away the hours. 🚇 1, 4: Schwedenplatz

Franziskanerplatz (E4) This picturesque square is graced by the Franciscan church of St Jerome (Hieronymus) and, near the fountain, one of the town's most charming coffeehouses, a tiny place aptly named Kleines Café, famous for its fried eggs. 🚇 1, 3: Stephansplatz

Winterpalais des Prinzen Eugen (E4) To thank Prince Eugène of Savoy (1663–1736) for his victory over the Turks, Leopold I let him call upon Austria's greatest architects to build a summer residence—the Belvedere—and this baroque winter palace. Begun by Fischer von Erlach in 1697, it was completed in 1724 by Hildebrandt. Today the palace serves as headquarters of the Finance Ministry. • Himmelpfortgasse 4 🚇 1, 3: Stephansplatz

Mozarthaus Vienna (E4) Wolfgang Amadeus Mozart (1756–91) and his wife Constanze lived in this pretty house from 1784 to 1787, and it was here that Mozart composed *The Marriage of Figaro* in 1785. It is his only surviving Viennese residence and was completely refurbished for his 250th anniversary in 2006. On four floors, the displays present Mozart's life and work. (If you also intend to visit the Haus der Musik, buy a Kombiticket.) • **Daily 10am–7pm** ☎512 17 91 • Domgasse 5 🚇 1, 3: Stephansplatz

Singerstrasse (E4) The doorway of the 18th-century Palais Neupauer-Breuner, No. 16, is flanked by two powerful Titans who appear to be holding up the building. Next door to the Gothic Elisabethenkirche, the seat of the German Knights' Order recalls the time of the Crusades. Its treasury includes relics of the Order, which is today a charitable organization. 🚇 1, 3: Stephansplatz

Rauhensteingasse (E4) The Steffl department store at No. 8 stands on the site of the house in which Mozart died; it was torn down in 1847. When Mozart moved in here with his wife Constanze in 1787, *The Marriage of Figaro* had just scored a great triumph in Prague. But the death of his father, long journeys, debts, intrigues and the Viennese public's bad reception for *Don Giovanni* and *Così fan tutte* left the composer completely exhausted. Sick and lonely, he died of a fever in the night from December 4 to 5, 1791. His body was buried in a mass paupers' grave in the St Marx cemetery. 🚇 1, 3: Stephansplatz

Kärntner Strasse (D6–E4) Named after one of the nine federal states, this bustling pedestrian-zoned shopping street links Stephansplatz to the Opera House. It is lined with open-air cafés, fountains and lime trees. Many of the houses were built after World War II. At No. 37, the Gothic Malteserkirche was founded by the Order of Maltese Knights at the time of the Crusades and their wars against Arabs and Turks. J. & L. Lobmeyr's glassware shop at No. 26 was built in 1823 to serve the imperial court; it now houses a glassware museum. Further on in the direction of the Opera House is the monumental 19th-century Hotel Sacher, whose pastry shop produces the original chocolate Sacher-Torte. 🚇 1, 3: Stephansplatz

Annagasse (E5) St Anne's Church (Annakirche) dates back to the 15th century but has been modified. Inside, St Anne is portrayed in a sculpture with Mary and Jesus. There are several fine mansions on Annagasse—the 17th-century Palais Esterházy at the corner of Kärtnerstrasse, now housing a casino; Hildebrandt's 18th-century Palais Deybelhof (No. 8); and various monastic inns: the 17th-century Kremsmünsterhof (4), Mariazell (5), and baroque Herzogenburgerhof (6). Note the grand façade of the early-19th-century Haus Zum blauen Karpfen (House of the Blue Carp). 🚇 1, 3: Stephansplatz

Haus der Musik (E5) The Palais Erzherzog Karl houses the museum of the Vienna Philharmonic Orchestra. It presents an interactive display exploring the

world of sound, with a separate section devoted to the great Viennese composers. You can give free rein to your fantasies and direct the orchestra—virtually. There's a great view of the Stephansdom from the 5th-floor café.
• Daily 10am–10pm ☎516 48 • Seilerstätte 30 Ⓤ 1, 3: Stephansplatz

Neuer Markt (D4) Heading along Kärntner Strasse towards the Opera, turn right on Donnergasse to Neuer Markt, the "new market" where the grain-merchants used to trade. In the middle of the square, the baroque Donnerbrunnen or Providentia Fountain was designed by Georg Raphael Donner in 1739. Four bronze statues symbolize the tributaries of the Danube: Enns, Traun, Ybbs and March. The originals, of lead, were replaced in 1873 and are now exhibited in the Belvedere's Baroque Museum. Among the handsome façades overlooking the square are those of the Palais Rauchmiller (No. 14) and a 19th-century merchant's house with a three-storey gable (10–11). Ⓤ 1, 3: Stephansplatz

Kapuzinerkirche and Kaisergruft (D4) The sober Capuchin Church was chosen by Emperor Matthias and wife Anna to serve from 1633 on as the Habsburgs' mausoleum. The crypts contain the remains of 12 emperors, 16 empresses and over 100 archdukes and their wives. The rococo sarcophagus of Maria Theresa and her husband François is particularly opulent. Among the great absentees: Karl V, buried in Spain; Marie-Antoinette, guillotined in Paris in 1793; her son Louis, who died in France in 1795; Archduke Franz Ferdinand and his wife; and the last emperor, Karl I, buried on Madeira. In 1989, 67 years after Karl I's death, almost all of Europe's royalty came here to the funeral of his widow Zita. • **Crypts daily 10am–6pm** ☎512 68 53 • Tegetthoffstrasse 2 Ⓤ 1, 3: Stephansplatz

Österreichisches Theatermuseum (D5) In 1710 Fischer von Erlach added a fine porch to this late-17th-century baroque palace. It was purchased by the Lobkowitz family in the mid-18th century; they were patrons of Beethoven and it was here that his Third "Eroica" Symphony was first performed, in 1803, and his Fourth in 1807. The palace houses the collections of the Austrian theatre museum. The Kindertheatermuseum organizes activities for children from 5 to 12. • **Tues–Sun 10am–6pm. Guided tours by appointment.** ☎525 24 34 60
• Palais Lobkowitz, Lobkowitzplatz 2 Ⓤ U1, 3: Stephansplatz

WALKING TOUR: CITY CENTRE

From the **Börse** (Stock Exchange), built in the wake of the stockmarket crash of 1873, head east on Wipplingerstrasse to Josef Hackhofer's Jugendstil **Hohe Brücke** and turn left on Schwertgasse, where the lofty 14th-century Gothic church of **Maria am Gestade** rises above a monumental staircase. East of the church, turn right on Stoss im Himmel past the **Altes Rathaus** to cross Wipplingerstrasse with its grand baroque **Böhmische Hofkanzlei** (Bohemian Chancellery). Füttergasse leads to **Judenplatz**, centre of the old Jewish ghetto with its statue of Gotthold Ephraim Lessing pointing now to a stark new Shoah monument and museum.

South of the square, **Parisergasse** passes two chic bistros, Bodega Marquès and Stern, to the little Schulhof square with its Clock Museum. Double back on **Kurrentgasse** to admire the ornate façades of its 18th-century houses. Leave Judenplatz on Jordangasse and turn right on Wipplingerstrasse to bustling **Hoher Markt**. With their splendid Gelateria ice cream parlour, latterday Romans pay tribute to forefathers who built the ancient forum here.

Walk north on Judengasse to **Ruprechtskirche**, Vienna's oldest church. Seitenstettengasse leads past the modern **Synagogue** (No. 4) into the notorious "Bermuda Triangle" of bars where ravers disappear at night. Turn right on Rabensteig and left on Fleischmarkt to enter **Heiligenkreuzer Hof** convent (through Köllnerhofgasse and then Grashofgasse 3). Exit into pretty **Schönlaterngasse**, with some fine old houses (6 and 7) and Hermann Czech's handsome Wunder Bar (8). The street owes its name to the "beautiful lantern" at No. 6. Turn left on Sonnenfelsgasse to the Baroque **Jesuitenkirche** and Akademie der Wissenschaften (Science Academy), once a boarding school where Schubert was a choirboy.

CITY CENTRE 35

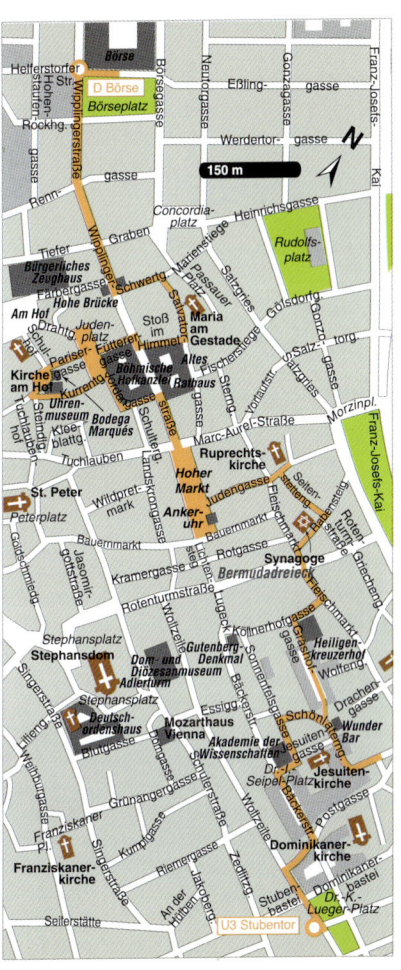

CITY CENTRE'S HISTORIC BEGINNINGS

Away from the crowds, visit the 1st District's historic sites tucked away between the Stock Exchange and the school where Schubert sang in the choir.

Start:
🚊 1, 2 Börse

Finish:
🅄 3 Stubentor

Time:
A good hour

THE HOFBURG

The strategic heart of the empire expanded in proportion to the growth of the Habsburgs' power. The buildings of the Hofburg express the most varying styles: Gothic, Renaissance, baroque, rococo and neoclassical.

THE DISTRICT AT A GLANCE

SIGHTS

Architecture
Neue Hofburg...........38
Redoutensaal 38
Österreichische Nationalbibliothek ...38

Churches
Augustinerkirche......39

Entertainment
Winterreitschule ★....38

Museums
Kaiserappartements ★ 36
Silberkammer 36
Sisi Museum 37
Schatzkammer ★ 37
Völkerkundemuseum 38
Albertina ★ 39

WALKING TOUR 40

WINING AND DINING 87

Kaiserappartements (Hofburg map, D4) The entrance is beneath the Michaelerkuppel (dome). Tickets give access to the collections of silver and porcelain **(Silberkammer)**, the private apartments and the Sisi Museum—the Leopold Wing is closed to the public as it is the seat of the President of the Republic. Tours begin with the private apartments of Franz Joseph, a succession of 19 spacious chambers decorated with gilded stucco and tapestries, lit by sparkling Bohemian crystal chandeliers. In the long dining room, its walls lined with Flemish tapestries, the table is set for a family dinner. Imagine the emperor who would accompany his guests after a meal to the Cercle reception room or the smoking parlour with its Brussels tapestries. Official audiences took place twice weekly, Franz Joseph standing behind his desk to hear the dolences of his petitioners. In Napoleonic Empire style, the conference room reserved for his ministers is next to his dressing room. His sleeping quarters are quite modest by comparison: portraits of his wife Elisabeth and mother Sophie hang above a simple iron bed. The apartments of Elisabeth are in the adjoining Amalienburg, a 16th-century Renaissance building. Here, in addition to her bedroom

THE HOFBURG

The Michaelertor is the grandiose entrance gate to the Hofburg.

and living room, you can see a gymnasium, complete with wooden exercise apparatus fixed to the ceiling. When Sissi was in the palace, the royal couple dined in the splendid Grand Salon. Memorabilia of the last imperial couple, Karl I and Zita, are displayed in the rooms occupied by Tsar Alexander I during the Congress of Vienna. The **Sisi Museum**, devoted entirely to the life of Empress Sissi, takes up six rooms of the Stephans-Appartements. • Daily 9am–5pm, last entry 4.30pm; July and August daily 9am–5.30pm, last entry 5pm. Audioguides available in several languages, free of charge. Guided tours several times daily. ☎ 533 75 70 • Michaelerplatz 1 **U** 3: Herrengasse ⇌ 1, 2, D, J: Burgring

Schatzkammer (Hofburg map, D4) The Schweizertor, a superb Renaissance gateway (1552), opens onto the Schweizerhof courtyard. Here, the Treasury displays the imperial jewels: the crown of the Holy Roman Empire created in the 10th century; the Austrian imperial crown of the 17th century and the treasure of the Burgundians (15th century). Among the numerous other precious gems, reliquaries and works of art is the magnificent necklace of the Order of the Golden Fleece founded in 1429. • **Daily (except Tues) 10am–6pm** ☎525240

Neue Hofburg (D5) Part of the collections of the Kunsthistorisches Museum are displayed in the colonnade of the newest section of the Hofburg. The Ephesus Museum, exhibiting finds from Austrian excavations in Anatolia at the beginning of the 20th century, is a must for archaeology buffs. There's an exhibition of armour and weapons in the Hofjagd- und Rüstkammer, as well as a collection of historic musical instruments. The **Völkerkundemuseum** (Ethnology Museum) assembles more than 200,000 objects from all over the world, among them the collection of Captain Cook, which Emperor Franz I purchased in London in 1806. Particularly noteworthy is the elaborate feather head-dress and costume of the Aztec emperor Montezuma, killed by the troops of conquistador Hernan Cortes in 1520. • **Wed–Mon 10am–6pm** ☎525240

Winterreitschule (D4) This section of the imperial stables is reserved for the Spanish Riding School. The famous performances of the Lippizaner horses take place in a splendid dazzling white hall with a colonnade designed by Fischer von Erlach in 1735. The hall also served as a setting for many ceremonial occasions, notably in the Congresses of Vienna, and Beethoven directed an orchestra of more than 1000 musicians for a concert here in 1814. • **Performances mostly Fri 7pm, Sat and Sun 11am (except July and August). For exact dates see www.srs.at. Horse training with music Tues–Sat 10am–noon.** ☎533 90 31 10 • Michaelerplatz 1

Redoutensaal (D4) The emperor held illustrous masquerade balls in the Redouten Hall, a grand ballroom built in 1760. And aristocratic delegates to the Congress of Vienna danced here for weeks on end to celebrate victory over Napoleon. It has been restored to its former grandeur after the devastating fire of 1992 that also practically destroyed the stables of the Riding School.

Österreichische Nationalbibliothek (D4) The national library is one of the most important in the world, including the books and incunabula of the imperial library dating back to the 14th century. The main entrance offers a splendid view over the surrounding monuments (museums, parliament, city hall). Used today for exhibitions and concerts, the great hall on the first floor (Prunksaal) is a masterly baroque design (1726) by Fischer von Erlach. The ceiling painting in the dome depicts the apotheosis of Karl VI. ☎534 10 • Josefsplatz 1

Augustinerkirche (D5) The former imperial parish church (14th century), was used for weddings. A painting in the left aisle of the Virgin of the Snows, patron saint of the House of Habsburg, was said to grow darker when the dynasty was threatened by misfortune. A fine marble monumental tomb (1805) was designed by Antonio Canova for Archduchess Marie Christine, a daughter of Maria Theresa. In a crypt near the Loretta Chapel—known with characteristic sentimentality as the Herzgrüftl (Little Heart Crypt)—54 silver urns contain the hearts of the Habsburgs. That of the Duke of Reichstadt (son of Napoleon) is decorated by a French tri-color ribbon. • Daily 10am–6pm, Sun 1–6pm Visits by appointment ☎533 70 99 • Augustinerstrasse 3

Albertina (D5) The world's greatest graphic art collection includes hundreds of thousands of drawings, water colours and prints by such masters as Leonardo da Vinci, Dürer, Raphael, Michelangelo and Rembrandt, but also 20th-century artists like Klimt and Schiele, in changing exhibitions. The Habsburgs' state rooms are also open to the public. • Daily 10am–6pm; Wed to 9pm ☎534 83 • Albertinaplatz 1

HIGH SCHOOL

The white Lipizzaner horses of the Spanish Riding School leave the stables early in the morning for rehearsals across the street. The school dates back to the 16th century. Archduke Karl, brother of Maximilian II, owned lands in north Slovenia. He set up a stud farm in Lipica, near Trieste, to cross-breed Berber and Arabian horses brought from Spain. In 1920 part of it was moved to Piber, near Graz. The horses begin training at the age of 4, when their coats start turning white.

WALKING TOUR: WEST OF THE HOFBURG

To the right of the grand neo-Renaissance **Burgtheater**, enter the **Volksgarten**, Vienna's oldest public park (1809), through a side entrance. and turn left to fountains and flower gardens framing the ornate white marble monument to "Sissi"—Empress Elisabeth. In the centre of the park is the **Theseus Temple**. South of this 19th-century replica of Athens' Theseion are a monument to poet Franz Grillparzer (1791–1872) and a couple of popular cafés and beer-gardens.

Exit through the park's main gate on Dr-Karl-Renner-Ring and head south past the **Parliament** to turn right on Volksgartenstrasse. Opposite the old **Café Raimund** (Museumstrasse 9), the **Volkstheater** presents an avant-garde counterpart to the prestigious Burgtheater. On Neustiftgasse, pass Fischer von Erlach's baroque **Palais Trautson**, built 1712 for Hungarian guard-officers and now the Justice Ministry. Neustiftgasse has some fine **Jugendstil buildings**, Dreifaltigkeitshof (6/8) and two apartment buildings by Otto Wagner: No 40 at the corner of Döblergasse, and his home and last workshop next door, Döblergasse 4.

Double back and turn right at Kellermanngasse past Café Nepomuk, entering the cobblestone **St-Ulrichsplatz**. Around its buttermilk baroque church (1724) are several 18th-century houses, No.2 boasting a handsome inner courtyard. Gourmets reserve a table at the renowned **Gasthaus Spatzennest** (☎ 526 16 59).

Turn left on Burggasse and right on Stiftgasse into the colourful **Spittelberg** neighbourhood, once a notorious "red light district" and now a lively quarter for artists and tavern-hoppers. **Amerlinghaus** (Stiftgasse 8) is the hub of its cultural activities. Stroll around gaily painted houses, shops and galleries on Schrankgasse, Spittelberggasse, Gutenberggasse and Kirchberggasse.

THE HOFBURG 41

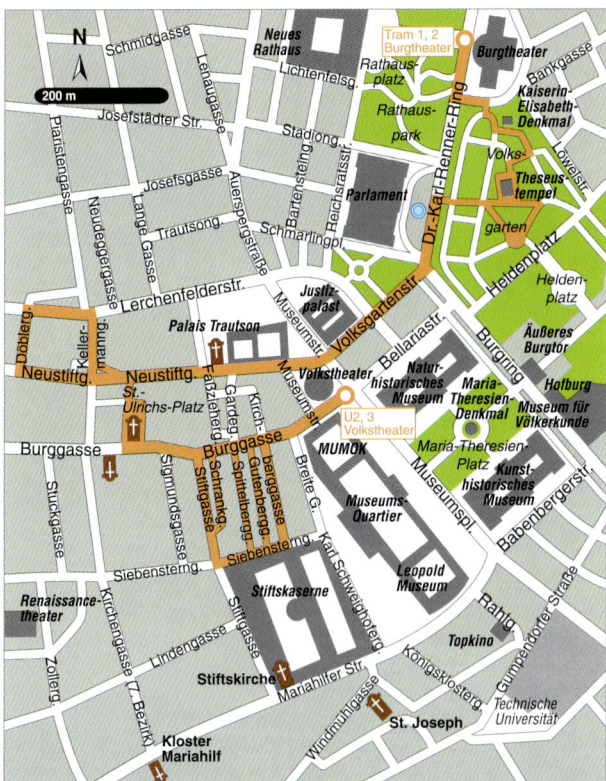

THE PEOPLE'S VIENNA
Leave the pomp of Hofburg and Burgtheater to explore "the people's Vienna" reaching from the Volksgarten to the refurbished Spittelberg neighbourhood.

Start: 1, 2 Burgtheater
Finish: U2, 3 Volkstheater
Time: about 1 hour

THE RING

Our description of monuments along the broad semi-circular boulevard called Ringstrasse goes anti-clockwise, from the University to the Danube Canal. U-Bahn 2 goes round it from the canal to Karlsplatz.

THE DISTRICT AT A GLANCE

SIGHTS

Architecture
Universität 42
Neues Rathaus ★ 43
Burgtheater ★ 43
Parlament 44
Staatsoper ★ 46
Postsparkasse 47

Churches
Votivkirche ★ 42

Entertainment
Stadtpark ★ 46
Urania 47

Museums
Beethoven Pasqualatihaus ★ 42
Naturhistorisches Museum 45

Kunsthistorisches Museum ★ 45
MuseumsQuartier ★ .46
MAK 46

WALKING TOUR 48

WINING AND DINING 87

Universität (C2) The University of Vienna was founded in 1365. You can still visit the original Science Academy (Akademie der Wissenschaften, Dr-Ignaz-Seipel-Platz 2). In 1883, architect Heinrich Ferstel was commissioned to build the new University in neo-Renaissance style; it has 72,000 students today. • Dr Karl-Lueger-Ring 1 **U** 2: Schottentor

Votivkirche (C2) Another major work by Ferstel, the neo-Gothic church behind the University was commissioned by Archduke Maximilian as thanks for his brother's escape from an assassination attempt. Maximilian became Emperor of Mexico and was killed by Mexican revolutionaries in 1867, 12 years before the church was completed. Inside is the tomb of Count Niklas Salm, commander in chief at the first Turkish siege of 1529. • Tues–Sat 9am–1pm and 4–6.30pm; Sun 9am–1.30pm ☎406 11 92 • Rooseveltplatz 8 **U** 2: Schottentor

Beethoven-Pasqualatihaus (C3) Ludwig van Beethoven (1770–1827) came to Vienna in 1792, was a student of Haydn and soon found recognition among

Attentive audience in the plush and gilded magnificence of the Staatsoper.

his fellow musicians and the Vienna public. This house, now a museum, frequently served as Beethoven's home between 1804 and 1815. He composed here the opera *Fidelio* and his 5th and 6th Symphonies. • **Tues–Sun 10am–1pm and 2–6pm; closed on several public holidays** ☎ 535 89 05 • **Mölkerbastei 8** 🇺 2: Schottentor

Neues Rathaus (C3) The New City Hall is the seat of regional and city government. It was built in 1883 in neo-Gothic style by Swabian architect Friedrich von Schmidt. In the basement is the popular Wiener Rathauskeller restaurant. Outside, the square hosts the Christmas market in winter and an opera film festival in summer. • **Guided tours Mon, Wed, Fri (except during council meetings and public holidays) at 1pm** ☎ 525 50 • **Rathausplatz 1** 🇺 2: Rathaus

Burgtheater (C3) Empress Maria Theresa founded the first Burgtheater in one of the Hofburg's ballrooms. In 1874, construction began on a new Burgtheater,

IMPERIAL GRANDEUR

The Ringstrasse is one of Emperor Franz Joseph's great achievements. Impressed on his visit to London by Britain's Great Exhibition of 1851, he wanted to give his own capital a whole new look. From Christmas 1857, he had the city walls razed to make way for a broad boulevard. The Ring was bordered by numerous public buildings in different styles. The architecture was to correspond to the function. This "historicism" gave Vienna a distinctly bourgeois appearance. To pay for the public works, remaining prime building sites on the Ring were sold to aristocrats for their town mansions.

opposite the Neues Rathaus. It opened in 1888. The building designed by Carl Hasenauer and Gottfried Semper in Italian Renaissance style was destroyed in 1945 but fully restored after the war. • **Guided tours Sept–June at 3 pm (lasting 1 hr); main entrance near the cash desks.** ☎514 44 4140 • Dr-Karl-Lueger-Ring 2 🅄 2: Rathaus

Parlament (C4) Designed by the Danish architect Theophil Hansen, the edifice was completed in 1884. Having studied in Athens, Hansen chose

the neoclassical style for the parliament building. It was here that the dual monarchy was dissolved and the founding of the republic proclaimed. The bicameral parliamentary system has a national council (Nationalrat) elected for four years and the federal council (Bundesrat) comprising representatives of the nine federal states. • **Guided tours** (except when parliament in session) Mid Sept–mid July Mon,Tues 10am, 1am, 2pm, 3pm, 4pm; Wed, Thurs also at 5pm; Fri also at 1pm; Sat 10am, 11am, noon, 1pm ☎401 10 24 00 • Dr-Karl-Renner-Ring 3 U 2: Lerchenfelder Strasse

Naturhistorisches Museum (C4–5) After the Burgtheater, architects Hasenauer and Semper tackled two buildings in Italian Renaissance style, the Natural History and History of Art museums, flanking the monument to Maria Theresa. Departments of the Natural History Museum are devoted to prehistory, anthropology, mineralogy, zoology and palaeontology. The particularly fine collection of precious stones includes a topaz weighing 117 kg (257 pounds). Also famous is the 25,000-year-old limestone statuette known as the Venus of Willendorf, a fertility symbol unearthed at the beginning of the 20th century in Lower Austria. • **Daily** (except Tues) 9am–6.30pm, Wed to 9pm ☎521 770 • Maria-Theresien-Platz U 2 Volkstheater or MuseumsQuartier, 3: Volkstheater ⚡ 1, 2 D or J: Dr-Karl-Renner-Ring

Kunsthistorisches Museum (C5) The History of Art Museum displays the Habsburgs' collections assembled over the ages and finally opened to the public by Franz Joseph at the end of the 19th century. The rich collection of paintings is up on the first floor. It exhibits Flemish, Dutch, Italian, French, Spanish, English and German masters, including Arcimboldo, Brueghel, Dürer, Poussin, Rembrandt, Rubens, Raphael, Titian, Tintoretto, Velazquez (portraits of the Spanish royal family) and Vermeer, whose Allegory of Painting is one of the museums most prized possessions. On the ground floor are the Egyptian, Oriental, Greek and Roman art treasures and sculptures. The coin collection is on the second floor. • **Art gallery, Egyptian and Oriental collections, Antiquities:** daily (except Mon) 10am–6pm; Thurs to 9pm. Coins: daily (except Mon) 10am–6pm. Sculpture and objets d'art: ☎525 24 40 25 • Maria-Theresien-Platz U 2 Volkstheater or MuseumsQuartier, 3: Volkstheater ⚡ 1, 2 D or J: Dr-Karl-Renner-Ring

MuseumsQuartier (C5) Behind Fischer von Erlach's pink façade of the former Imperial stables, 316 m long, the spectacular new museum district comprises baroque buildings, new architecture, many different cultural institutions and museums, concert halls, dance centre, and other recreational facilities. For a full list, see www.mqw.at. The **Leopold Museum** houses a large collection of paintings and drawings by Egon Schiele, who died in 1918 aged 28. The black basalt **Museum of Modern Art** (MUMOK), by architects Ortner & Ortner, displays modern and contemporary art, including paintings by Klee, Léger, Kandinsky, Magritte and Kokoschka, sculptures by Brancusi, Giacometti and Max Ernst. **ZOOM**: for all children from toddlers to 14 years old, exhibitions and interactive workshops. **Kunsthalle**: exhibition hall for contemporary art. • www.mqw.at • Leopold Museum daily 10am–6pm; Thurs to 9pm. ☎525 700 • MUMOK daily 10am–6pm, Thurs to 9pm ☎525 00 • ZOOM Children's Museum: open daily, each programme beginning at a specific time. Reservation advised. ☎524 79 08 • Kunsthalle Wien: daily 10am–7pm; Thurs to 10pm ☎521 890 • Museumsplatz 1 🅄 2: MuseumsQuartier

Staatsoper (D5) Franz Joseph commissioned August Sicard von Sicardsburg and Eduard van der Nüll to build the Opera House, a neo-Renaissance temple of lyrical art. At its opening in 1869, it came under violent attack from the Viennese who found it ugly and unworthy of the city's musical heritage. In 1945, it was badly damaged but restored to its former appearance and re-opened in 1955 with Beethoven's *Fidelio*. On the Thursday before Mardi Gras, the opera house is completely transformed for the traditional Opera Ball. • **Guided tours** ☎514 44 26 06 • Opernring 2 🅄 1, 2, 4: Karlsplatz 🚋 1, 2 D or J: Oper

Stadtpark (F4–5) Stretching across both banks of the Wien Fluss canal, the City Park was the first to be opened by the municipality, in 1862. The gilded monument of Strauss, the violin-playing Waltz King, is a favourite photo subject for tourists but other musicians are commemorated there, too. Concerts are held from Easter to October at the Kursalon bandstand near the park entrance. • Parkring 🅄 4: Stadtpark 🚋 1, 2: Weihburggasse

Museum für angewandte Kunst (MAK) (F4) The Museum of Applied Arts was built from 1867 to 1871. It is a show-place for the celebrated Wiener Werk-

The stark dark walls of MUMOK lend themselves to all kinds of imaginative exhibitions.

stätte (Vienna Workshops), but also for collections of handicraft and design from the world over. • Daily (except Mon) 10am–6pm, Thurs till midnight. Sat free admission ☎ 71 13 60 • Stubenring 5 **U** 3: Stubentor or 4 Wien Mitte/Landstrasse ⇌ 1, 2: Stubentor or 1, 2, 3, 7, 15 Wien Mitte/Landstrasse

Postsparkasse (F3) Completed in 1912, the Imperial and Royal Post Office Savings Bank building is a masterpiece of Otto Wagner in glass, concrete and steel. • Mon, Thurs 8.30am–5.30pm; Tues, Wed 8.30am–3.30pm; Sat 10am––5pm • Georg-Coch-Platz **U** 1, 4: Schwedenplatz or 3: Stubentor ⇌ 1, 2: Julius-Raab-Platz

Urania (F3) Two façades of this Jugendstil building look onto the Danube Canal. Designed by Max Fabiani (1910), it houses a cinema, an observatory and a puppet theatre. ☎ 712 61 91 • Uraniastrasse 1 **U** 1, 4: Schwedenplatz or 3: Stubentor ⇌ 1, 2: Julius-Raab-Platz

WALKING TOUR: THE RING

Built in 1898 to harmonize with the gardens and river, Otto Wagner's **Stadtbahnstation Stadtpark** is itself worth a look before taking the stairs down to the **River Wien**. Walk along the riverbank to the first bridge with stairs leading up to the park. To the left, among the park's many statues celebrating the town's musicians is the **monument to Johann Strauss**. The Waltz King *(Walzerkönig)* plays his violin facing the **Kursalon** concert-café offering coffee, pastries and public waltz competitions. Along the Parkring side of the gardens, stroll past monuments commemorating other local composers, including Franz Lehar and Schubert.

From the park's Stubenring exit, turn right past the imposing redbrick **Museum für angewandte Kunst** (Applied Arts Museum, MAK). Two great choices here for coffee: the museum's avant-garde **Österreicher im MAK Café** or across the street, the more traditional **Café Prückel** (Stubenring 24). Continue to the gigantic Ministerium für Wirtschaft und Arbeit (Economy and Labour Ministry), fronted by the equally forbidding equestrian **statue of Field Marshal Radetzky**. The 19th-century war hero points across the Ring to Georg-Coch Platz and Otto Wagner's Jugendstil masterpiece **Postsparkasse** (Postal Savings Bank, 1906). Enjoy a quiet stroll around the magically lit interior as part of your walk.

Back on the Stubenring, turn left to walk around Julius-Raab Platz to the lighthouse-like tower of the **Urania**, now a cinema with a rooftop observatory. For a good view of the **Danube Canal**, cross the Aspernbrücke and end your walk on an ultra-modern note at the handsome **Uniqa Tower** office building designed in 2004 by Heinz Neumann.

THE RING 49

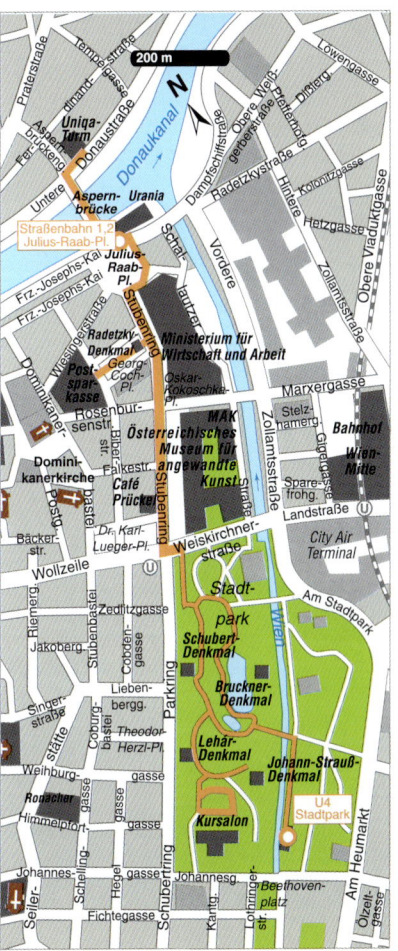

THE OTHER SIDE OF THE RING

From the pleasant Stadtpark, where the Viennese still indulge their taste for pastry and waltzes, make your way to the pretty if not-so-blue Danube Canal.

Start: U4 Stadtpark

Finish: 1, 2 Julius-Raab Platz

Time: about 45 minutes

KARLSPLATZ AND THE BELVEDERE

A walk from the Opera over the Ring shows a good cross-section of Viennese architecture: the 19th-century Hotel Imperial, the characteristic Jugendstil Karlsplatz subway station, and the baroque Karlskirche. Further south is the Belvedere with its splendid gardens and museums.

THE DISTRICT AT A GLANCE

SIGHTS

Architecture
Karlsplatz-
Pavillons ★ 53
Hotel Imperial 53
Belvedere ★ 54

Churches
Karlskirche 50

Entertainment
Musikverein ★ 51
Künstlerhaus 51

Museums
Wien Museum
Karlsplatz 50

Secession 53
Akademie der
bildenden Künste.....54

WALKING TOUR 56

WINING AND DINING 89

Karlskirche (E7) Vienna's finest baroque church is dedicated to St Charles Borromeo, Bishop of Milan (1538–84). His statue crowning the pediment was sculpted by Lorenzo Mattielli. St Charles had shown great courage when Milan was struck by the plague, and after Vienna was hit by the same disaster, in 1713, his example prompted Emperor Karl VI to have this grandiose monument built by Johann and son Joseph Fischer von Erlach. With a formidable copper dome flanked by two triumphal pillars covered in spiral bas-reliefs, it is one of the city's great landmarks. An inside panoramic elevator takes you up to a height of 32.5 m to see the ceiling paintings up close. Climb a little higher for a view over the city. • Mon–Sat 9am–12.30pm and 1–6pm; Sun and holidays noon–5.45pm • Karlsplatz U 1, 2, 4: Karlsplatz

Wien Museum Karlsplatz (E6) The Vienna History Museum traces the city's development from prehistoric times to the present. • Daily (except Mon) 9am–6pm; free admission Sun ☎505 87 470 • Karlsplatz U 1, 2, 4: Karlsplatz

A sunflowered archway on one of Otto Wagner's pavilions on Karlsplatz.

Musikverein (E6) This is the home of the Vienna Philharmonic. The building was commissioned by the Gesellschaft der Musikfreunde (Society of Music Lovers) from the Danish architect Theophil Hansen, who also designed the Austrian Parliament and the Academy of Fine Arts. Behind its distinctive ochre façade, completed in 1869, are two concert halls frequented by some 700,000 music-lovers every year: the Brahmssaal for chamber music and the famous Goldener Saal, known throughout the world for the Philharmonic's New Year's Day concert. The gilded caryatids are repainted each summer. • **Box office Mon–Fri 9am–8pm; Sat 9am–1pm (July–Aug Mon–Fri 9am–noon).** ☎505 81 90 • Bösendorferstrasse 12 Ⓤ 1, 2, 4: Karlsplatz ⇌ 1, D, J: Kärntner Ring; ⇌ 2, 62, 65: Opernring

Künstlerhaus (E6) A historic building now housing a modern exhibition hall (k/haus). Cinema, restaurant and live events. • **Daily 10am–6pm, Thurs to 9pm** ☎587 96 63 • Karlsplatz 5 Ⓤ 1, 2, 4: Karlsplatz

Hotel Imperial (E6) Vienna's most distinguished hotel lives up to its name—guests are treated like emperors. Built as a palace for the Duke of Württemberg in 1865, it was transformed to a grand hotel for the World Exhibition of 1873. • **Kärntner Ring 16** 🅄 **1, 2, 4: Karlsplatz** 🚊 **1, 2: Schwarzenbergplatz**

Karlsplatz-Pavillons (D6) At the beginning of the 20th century, Otto Wagner was commissioned to build bridges and stations for the new municipal railway, part underground, part ground-level. He tackled the job with great enthusiasm, putting his personal stamp on the city. The success of his enterprise is admired to this day. One of the pavilions, superbly decorated in marble and gilt, leads to the Karlsplatz subway. The pavilion on the west side is used by the Vienna Museum for changing exhibitions. Other surviving stations and bridges can be seen on line 3 (Schönbrunn station) and along the Gürtel ("beltway", line U6). • **Karlsplatz** 🅄 **1, 2, 4: Karlsplatz**

Secession (D6) Designed in 1898 by Joseph Maria Olbrich, a disciple of Otto Wagner, this white landmark cubic building topped by an open-work dome broke with Vienna's academic traditions and the ponderous, pompous official style of the times. An inscription in gold over the entrance sums up the philosophy of the Secession movement: "To each age, its art, to art its freedom". In the basement is the Beethoven Frieze (1902) by Gustav Klimt. It measures 26 m (85 ft) in length and honours the composer and his 9th Symphony. Today the Secession building is used for changing exhibitions

◀ *The filigree dome of the Secession consists of 3,000 gilden laurel leaves. The irreverent Viennese call it the "golden cabbage".*

of modern art. • Daily (except Mon) 10am–6pm, Thurs to 8pm. Tours Sat 3pm, Sun 11am ☎587 53 07 • Friedrichstrasse 12 **U** 1, 2, 4: Karlsplatz

Akademie der bildenden Künste (D6) Contemporary artists develop their talents in the Academy of Fine Arts, designed in 1876 by Theophil Hansen, architect of the Parliament and Musikverein. The art gallery, exhibiting works of Flemish and Dutch masters of the 17th century, is well worth a visit. You will see paintings by Rembrandt, Rubens, Van Meytens and Vermeyen, but also the literally fantastic *Day of Judgment* by Hieronymus Bosch. Painted in oils on wood panels, the great triptych (1504–08) gives a colourful depiction of the fallen angels and hell fires burning, the creation of Eve, and the momentous events of the Garden of Eden. • Daily (except Mon and certain public holidays) 10am–6pm ☎588 16-225 • Schillerplatz 3 **U** 1, 2, 4: Karlsplatz

Belvedere (F7) After France's Louis XIV had refused him command of a regiment, Prince Eugène of Savoy entered the service of Emperor Leopold I and soon distinguished himself as a successful field commander. Thanks to his victory over the Turks in the Balkans, Austria was able to recapture Hungary. Leopold rewarded the prince generously with lands just outside Vienna city centre. Eugène's festivities found an appropriately opulent setting in the Upper Belvedere completed in 1721 by Lukas von Hildebrandt in French baroque style. After his death in 1736, his niece sold the two Belvedere palaces to the emperor. Sixty years later, the daughter of Louis XVI and Marie-Antoinette spent three years here when released from prison in Paris. At the end of the 18th century, the art gallery was installed in the Belvedere. During the French occupation of 1809, it served as an army hospital and the director of the Louvre had 401 paintings transferred to Paris. Most were returned to Austria in 1815, after the Congress of Vienna. From 1894, the palace was the residence of the ill-fated Archduke Franz Ferdinand. The Austrian State Treaty was signed in the Marble Hall on May 15, 1955, re-establishing the independence and neutrality of the country.

The **Unteres Belvedere** (Lower Belvedere) served as Prince Eugène's summer residence; he settled there after the capture of Belgrade in 1716. The courtyard is reached through a handsome gateway. The palace now houses the **Baroque Museum**, exhibiting works by major Austrian painters and sculptors of the 17th to 19th centuries. Its many ceremonial halls include the Marble Gallery (Marmorgalerie), the Gold Cabinet (Goldkabinett), where a statue of Prince Eugène is reflected an infinite number of times in huge gold-framed mirrors, and the Hall of Grotesques (Groteskensaal), with an intriguing collection of grimacing heads by Franz Xaver Messerschmidt (1736–83). The walls are painted with frescoes by Jonas Drentwett depicting mythical beasts inspired by murals of ancient Rome. In the adjoining Orangerie, the **Museum of Medieval Austrian Art** includes some fine altar-paintings of the 15th century.

Between the Lower and Upper Belvederes are the elegant gardens laid out with statues, fountains and water basins by the Parisian landscape architect Dominique Girard. Entrance to the **Oberes Belvedere** (Upper Belvedere) is through an elegant gateway flanked by two lions. The rococo décor reflected in the ornamental pond recalls the grand masked balls and fireworks displays which Prince Eugène loved to stage for his guests. Since 1953, the Upper Belvedere has housed the **Austrian Gallery of the 19th and 20th Centuries**. You'll find 20th-century works on the ground floor, the Secession on the first floor and the 19th century and Biedermeier period on the second floor. In the central Sala Terrena, four great white Atlantes by Lorenzo Matielli hold up the vaulted ceiling, the Gustav Klimt collection includes his famous *Kiss* painting, and there are works by Egon Schiele.

• Museums open daily 10am– 6pm; for guided tours ☎79 55 70
• Prinz-Eugen-Strasse 27 **U** 1: Südtirolerplatz; ⬌ O, 18: Südbahnhof or D: Schloss Belvedere or Am Heumarkt

WALKING TOUR: NASCHMARKT

From the gleaming landmark of Joseph Maria Olbrich's **Secession** building (Friedrichstrasse 12), cross Getreidemarkt to **Theater an der Wien** at Linke Wienzeile N°6. Like film stars on Hollywood's Sunset Boulevard, great musicians now have their stars embedded in the pavement of Vienna's Music Mile *(Musikmeile)*, starting here with Beethoven, Mozart and actor-librettist Emanuel Schikaneder. Walk back to Millöckergasse and turn left to the theatre's original neoclassical façade (1797) with its sculpture of Schikaneder as Papageno playing the Magic Flute over the entrance.

Turn left on Lehargasse where a redbrick wall is still scarred with bullet holes from the end of World War II marked by a plaque commemorating *Wunden der Erinnerung* ("Wounds to Remember"). Lehargasse continues to Gumpendorferstrasse and **Café Sperl**, a monument among Vienna's coffeehouses with a tree-shaded terrace added to its famous billiard-table interior.

Double back to turn right down Girardigasse to the **Naschmarkt**. Jugendstil roofs and glazing shelter market stalls and Mediterranean and Balkan restaurants in a bazaar-like atmosphere cheerfully reinforced by its Turkish vendors. On Saturdays the Naschmarkt expands to include a flea market. Stalls spill over the pavements and you can happily rummage for bric-a-brac, china, old clothes and curios. Along the market's north side on **Linke Wienzeile** are two splendid examples of Otto Wagner's Jugendstil architecture, No. 38 decorated with medallions, No. 40 the **Majolikahaus** with a colourful ceramic-tiled façade.

On the market's south side, **Kettenbrückengasse U-Bahn Station** (1899) shows a more utilitarian but still elegant side of Wagner's talent. West of the station, you can see the **River Wien** before it runs underground, overlooked here by the garden of the superb Jugendstil **Café Rüdigerhof** (Hamburgerstrasse 20), a relaxing place to nasch or nosh, not just for its cabaret artist habitués.

KARLSPLATZ AND THE BELVEDERE 57

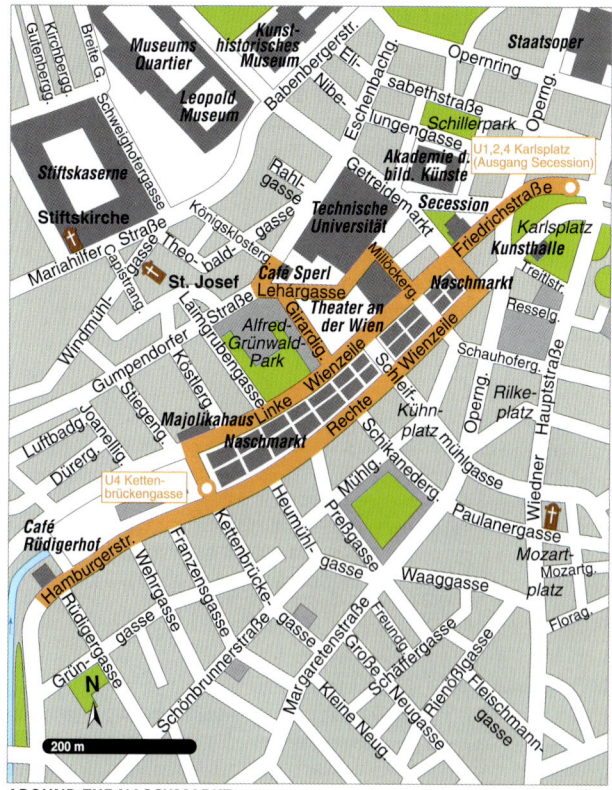

AROUND THE NASCHMARKT

Stroll around Vienna's most popular and most colourful street-market (closed Sunday), flanked by several cultural and architectural landmarks.

Start: 🚇1, 2, 4 Karlsplatz (Secession exit) **Finish:** 🚇4 Kettenbrückengasse
Time: about 40 minutes

VIENNA FOR CHILDREN

The city of Vienna puts a lot of energy and imagination into making a child's stay here enjoyable. From the outset, a tourist office guide shows where the priorities are: *Für Familienhäupter und deren Eltern* (For Heads of Family and their Parents). Your kids will have a wide choice of things they will be dying to do. With rare exceptions, English-language tours are available at the following attractions.

Schönbrunn Palace. At the end of the special children's palace tour there's a chance to dress up in the costumes of princes and princesses. The first-rate Marionette Theatre stages such full-scale shows as *Aladdin* or *The Magic Flute*. Or you may prefer to let the kids get lost in the park's maze and labyrinth *(Irrgarten und Labyrinth)*. Information ☎8111 3239, www.schoenbrunn.at/en/site/publicdir/.

Hofburg. Girls love the new **Sisi Museum**, devoted to the Empress Elisabeth's adventures, costumes, extravagant hairdos and beauty secrets. Behind the Hofburg in the Burggarten is the **Butterfly House** *(Schmetterlingshaus)*, an exotic delight.

Museums here prove they can really be fun. Housed in the MuseumsQuartier, pride of place goes to the kids' own **Zoom Kindermuseum** with four different attractions to cater for all ages: **Zoom-Ocean** for the very youngest; **Zoom-Studio** for budding artists to try their hand at painting and sculpture; **Zoom-Exhibition** to make hands-on contact with art museum exhibits and **Zoom-Lab** to learn the latest experiments in information technology and other state-of-the art techniques (☎524 7908, www.kindermuseum.at). **MUMOK**, the MuseumsQuartier's modern art museum, introduces children to the mysteries and excitement of avant-garde art. Here they can produce their own music or theatre (☎525 00 1313, www.mumok.at). Even the august **Kunsthistorisches Museum** has special tours for children, showing them not only the beloved Bruegels, but also Egyptian mummies and exhibits on the life of children in Ancient Greece and Rome ☎5252 4416. Fans of the more fanciful art of Friedensreich Hundertwasser will enjoy the children's attractions at his **Kunst-HausWien**, with prizes offered for the best child artists' designs for their own KunstHaus (Untere Weissgerberstrasse 13, ☎712 0495). The **Technisches Museum** has lots of interactive programmes for children, including rides on a fire engine and workshops for 6 to 12-year-olds (Mariahilfer Strasse 212, ☎899 98 6000).

Spanish Riding School. This world famous attraction requires advance booking for its public performances by the beautiful white prancing Lipizzan horses (see p.38).

Haus des Meeres (House of the Sea) is a huge aquarium fashioned from what was once a *Flak-Turm*, a gigantic anti-aircraft tower built by the German Army in World War II. You can feed some formidable-looking sharks and piranhas, and even be shown how to stroke some really placid snakes.

At the ever-popular **Prater Park,** take a ride on the Riesenrad (giant ferris wheel), and ghost train, or rent some roller-blades.

Danube cruises between Vienna and the Wachau Valley offer special shows for children aboard the Pyringer-Zopper Fleet's good ship *MS Schlöggen* (☎588 800).

The **Donauinsel beaches** offer facilities for swimming and other water sports, including windsurfing, water-skiing and rowing.

Winter visitors can enjoy the lively and colourful **Christkindlmarkt** (Christmas Market) on Rathausplatz where, among many other attractions, children are shown how to make their own handicraft presents. From January to March, a 2000-sq-m rink is set up on Rathausplatz for ice-skating.

OUTER DISTRICTS

Vienna has countless museums and galleries; here we offer a selection of unusual places for lovers of music, architecture—or even psychoanalysis. And don't miss Schloss Schönbrunn, and its lovely park.

THE DISTRICTS AT A GLANCE

SIGHTS		
Architecture	**Atmosphere**	Freud Museum ★ 61
KunstHausWien ★ 60	Zentralfriedhof..........62	Schuberts Geburtshaus............62
Otto-Wagner-Villa....62	Schlosspark ★ 66	Wagenburg 66
Kirche am Steinhof...63	**Museums**	
Schönbrunn Palace ★ 63	Kriminalmuseum......60	**WALKING TOUR** 68
	Wiener Strassenbahnmuseum 60	**WINING AND DINING** 89
	Liechtenstein Museum ★ 61	

Kriminalmuseum (F1) The Museum of Crime is enlivened with original photos and grisly pieces of evidence. • Thurs–Sun 10am–5pm or by appointment ☎ 214 46 78 • Grosse Sperlgasse 24, 2nd district Ⓤ 2: Taborstrasse ⮂ N, 21: Taborstrasse Bus 5A: Karmeliterplatz

KunstHausWien (H3) The artist Friedensreich Hundertwasser created the bizarre design for this museum with glass, metal and pieces of ceramics. There are no straight lines, and everything seems slightly skewed. Despite its confusing style—or because of it—this small, private gallery is worth a visit. • Daily 10am–7pm ☎ 712 04 91 • Untere Weissgerberstrasse 1, 33rd district ⮂ N, O: Radetzkyplatz

Wiener Strassenbahnmuseum (off map by H6) The Vienna Tram Museum, located in former terminus of the Erdberg District, displays some 100 trams tracing the history of this mode of transport. The museum also organizes tours of the city in an old tramway. • Early May to early Oct, Sat, Sun and public

OUTER DISTRICTS 61

The Hundertwasser-Haus, a cheerful design for a Viennese apartment block in the 3rd district.

holidays 9am–4pm ☎ 7909 41800 • Ludwig-Koessler Platz, 3rd district 🅄 3 or 🚋 18: Schlachthausgasse

Sigmund Freud Museum (C1) Sigmund Freud lived in this house for 47 years, and it was here that he treated his patients. The rooms are full of memorabilia of his life and work, but the original couch has remained in the Hampstead home of his London exile. The father of psychoanalysis died in London in September 1939. • Oct–June daily 9am–5pm; July–Sept 9am–6pm ☎ 319 15 96 • Berggasse 19, 9th district 🅄 2: Schottentor or Schottenring; 4: Schottenring or Rossauer Lände 🚋 D: Schlickgasse or 37, 38, 40, 41: Schwarzspanierstrasse

Liechtenstein Museum (off map by C1) This baroque palace, with sumptuous interior decoration, displays one of the biggest private art collections (particularly paintings and bronzes) with masterpieces from the early Renaissance

HUNDERTWASSER

Friedrich Stowasser (1928–2000) altered his name to Friedensreich Hundertwasser in 1949, after three months of study at Vienna's Academy of Fine Arts. Inspired by nature, the changing patterns reflected in water, the rhythms of Arabic music, he favoured the use of vibrant, saturated primary colours, and was fascinated by the spiral. His aversion for planned architecture with strict lines led him to design buildings with unlevel floors and curving walls, topped by trees and houses with grass roofs where animals can graze.

to Romanticism (Raphael, Rubens, Van Dyck, Mantegna, and others). • Fri–Tues 10am–5pm ☎ 319 57 67 252 • Fürstengasse 1, 9th district Ⓤ 4: Rossauer Lände ⇌ D or Bus 40A: Bauernfeldplatz

Schuberts Geburtshaus (off map by C1) Franz Schubert spent his childhood in this house, which has been converted into a museum. The composer is remembered for his string quartets and Lieder. He died in 1828 at 31 and was buried, at his own request, near Beethoven. • Daily (except Mon) 10am–1pm and 2–6pm; Sun free admission ☎ 317 36 01 • Nussdorferstrasse 54, 9th district ⇌ 37, 38: Canisiusgasse

Zentralfriedhof (off map by F7) Among the many "celebrities" buried in this cemetery, musicians have pride of place: Beethoven, Brahms, Schubert, Strauss, alongside countless writers, architects and artists. Mozart is commemorated by a monument. To the left of the main entrance, the little Russian orthodox chapel with a single onion dome was completed in 1840. At the far end of the cemetery, the majestic **Dr-Karl-Lueger Church** (1910) was designed by Max Hegele, a student of Otto Wagner, and dedicated to a former mayor of Vienna. • Nov to Feb daily 8am–5pm; Mar, Apr, Sept, Oct 7am–6pm; May–Aug 7am–8pm ☎ 760 41 • Simmeringer Hauptstrasse 234, 11th district ⇌ 6, 71: Zentralfriedhof

Otto-Wagner-Villa (Fuchs-Villa) (off map by A7) Otto Wagner built this Jugendstil villa for himself in 1886. A pioneer of "fantastic realism", the

OUTER DISTRICTS 63

The Kirche am Steinhof has stunning stained-glass windows by Koloman Moser.

artist Ernest Fuchs saved it from demolition in 1963, adding bright colours and a goddess of fertility. • Mon–Fri 10am–4pm, Sat, Sun by appointment. Tours for groups of at least 10 persons Mon–Fri 10am–4pm ☎ 914 85 75 • Hüttelbergstrasse 26, 14th district **U** 4: Hütteldorf ≠ 49 then Bus 148 or 152 to Camping West

Kirche am Steinhof (off map by A7) The golden-domed church built by Wagner (1905–7) for the psychiatric hospital is a stunning example of Jugendstil, with beautiful stained-glass windows. • Guided tours in German Sat 3pm (lasting 50 min); for groups by appointment ☎ 910 60 11 204 • Baumgartner Höhe 1, 14th district **U** 4: Unter St Veit, then Bus 47A to Psychiatrisches Zentrum

Schönbrunn Palace (off map by B7) Like many monarchs of his time, Leopold I wanted his new palace to surpass the magnificence and grandeur of Louis XIV's Versailles. In 1683, the Turkish seige had left Schloss Schönbrunn in ruins and Johann Bernhard Fischer von Erlach was commissioned to build the new summer residence. Nonetheless, a first project was rejected as too ambitious and too costly. A "more modest" choice was made with only 1,441 rooms. Construction continued until 1730. In order to give her court more sumptuous surroundings, Maria Theresa had the palace expanded in 1750 according to the plans of Nicolaus Pacassi. Thus the interior rooms were given a new décor, gardens were landscaped and the Empress opened Europe's first zoo in 1752.

Schönbrunn's architecture marks the ascendancy of the more playfully exuberant rococo over the apparent rigour of the baroque style. The glowing "Schönbrunn Yellow" of the buildings was copied throughout the empire on villas and palaces. Marie-Antoinette spent her youth here. Napoleon made it his headquarters in 1805 and again in 1809. His son, the Duke of Reichstadt, died here in 1832. Franz Joseph was born in Schönbrunn in 1830 and it was here that he died in 1916.

The grand entrance gate, Meidlinger Tor, which Napoleon flanked with his two imperial eagle-crowned obelisks, leads to a vast court of honour, Ehrenhof, used as a military parade ground by Napoleon. On the right is a small rococo theatre where concerts are still held in the summer. Marie-Antoinette danced in this theatre when she was a child, and Napoleon attended performances here.

The apartments of Franz Joseph and Elisabeth as well as the 15 reception halls are in the palace's right wing. The rooms are richly furnished, draped with brocade, the walls decorated with baroque panelling in beige and gold and hung with gleaming lacquerware and mirrors. Audience rooms have wood panelling from the 18th century. Franz Joseph's study has been maintained in its original condition, with its richly upholstered furniture. The emperor worked here till the day he died.

The Breakfast Room is adorned with 26 flower medallions embroidered by the Archduchess of Austria, Holy Roman Empress Maria Theresa (1717–80), and her daughters. You will also see Empress Elisabeth's two dressing rooms, her bedroom and drawing rooms. The Yellow Drawing Room is next to the little Hall of Mirrors (Spiegelsaal) in which Mozart gave one of his first recitals at the age of 6, in 1762.

Maria Theresa held secret meetings in the Chinese Round Room (Chinesisches Rundkabinett): a table rose up from the floor with dinner ready prepared so no

A marble naiad in the Star Pool (Sternbassin) watches over the gardens of Schönbrunn Palace.

servants could eavesdrop on the conversations. In the Blue Chinese Room (Blauer Chinesischer Salon) the last Habsburg emperor, Karl I, signed his abdication decree on November 11, 1918.

The Halls of the Carousel and Horses lead to the grand Hall of Ceremonies in the palace's left wing. Notice the splendid rococo décor in the Vieux-Laques Room. The wood panelling of the Million Room is inlaid with 260 Indian and Persian miniatures, which cost 1 million florins. Beyond the bedroom of Franz Joseph's mother Sophie of Bavaria, a study and drawing-room are hung with portraits of Maria Theresa, her husband François of Lorraine and their 16 children. • Apr–Oct daily 8.30am–5pm; July, Aug to 6pm; Nov–Mar daily 8.30am–4.30pm. Guided or individual audioguide tours: Imperial Tour—22 state rooms in approx. 35 minutes; Grand Tour—40 state rooms in 50 minutes. Children's tours Sat, Sun 10.30am and 2.30pm. ☎ 811 13 239
• Schönbrunner Schlossstrasse 47, 13th district 🆄 4: Schönbrunn 🚆 10, 58: Schönbrunn

Wagenburg What was once the Spanish Riding School now houses the impressive collection of the Kutschenmuseum (coach museum). The rococo imperial coach of 1700 was drawn by eight white horses and used for weddings and coronations, the last occasion being that of the young Emperor Karl I in December 1916. • April–October daily 9am–6pm, November–March daily (except Mon) 10am–4pm ☎ 525 24-0

Schlosspark The great park covering 160 ha (65 acres) was open to all Viennese citizens; only the small gardens to the left and right of the palace were reserved for the imperial family. The park

was laid out in French style in the 17th century and re-landscaped from 1750 to 1780. Ferdinand von Hohenberg designed the grand neoclassical Gloriette portico in 1775, commemorating the 1757 victory over the Prussian army. The view looking over Schloss Schönbrunn with Vienna in the background makes the climb well worthwhile. At the foot of the Gloriette hill is the Neptune Fountain. Hohenberg also built the artificial Roman ruins in the park grounds. Visit the zoo, which, although modern, has kept some of its baroque-style enclosures, the Palm House and Desert House with its plants and animals. • **Open daily (free admission). Zoo (Tiergarten): daily from 9am. Garden architecture tour: Apr–Oct, every 2nd and 4th Sunday at 2.30pm**

WALKING TOUR: SCHÖNBRUNN-HIETZING

From the Kennedy Bridge spanning the River Wien, look back along the railway tracks to the domed **Hofpavillon**, the palace's original station (no longer in use) built by Otto Wagner in 1898 for Emperor Franz Joseph. Hietzinger Hauptstrasse leads to the main town-square, Am Platz, and the **Hietzinger Tor** entrance to **Schönbrunn Park**. Go straight ahead along Finstere Allee and take the first diagonal right. Skirt the **Sternbassin** fountain and continue on to the recently resurrected **Maze and Labyrinth** *(Irrgarten und Labyrinth)*.

Beyond the Maze, turn left to the monumental **Neptune Fountain**. Behind the fountain, the left-hand path zigzags up to the neoclassical **Gloriette** with its grand hilltop view over the palace and the city beyond—and a **café** where you can relax after your climb. At the bottom of the hill, turn left on Rustenallee alongside the **Tiergarten** (zoo) to the majestic steel and glass **Palmenhaus** erected by Franz Joseph's great bridge-builder, Ignaz Gridl.

From the Hietzinger Tor exit, turn left on Maxingstrasse, right on Trauttmannsdorfgasse and left again to enter Hietzing's **Gloriette Quarter** along Wattmanngasse. At No. 29, Ernst Lichtblau's **Schokoladehaus** (1914) earned its nickname from the horizontal bands of dark brown ceramic bas-reliefs of rustic motifs. Turn right into Tirolergasse and walk down to where it meets Gloriettegasse and the imposing **Villa Schopp** (1901) at no. 21/23—note an intriguing "look-out window" set at an angle in the porter's lodge. Walk up Trauttmannsdorffgasse to see Hans Dvorák's **Fürstenhof** (No. 50) with its elegantly projecting oriel windows, then return to Gloriettegasse. Turn right to **Villa Skywa-Primavesi** (14/16), a masterpiece by Josef Hoffmann (1913).

OUTER DISTRICTS 69

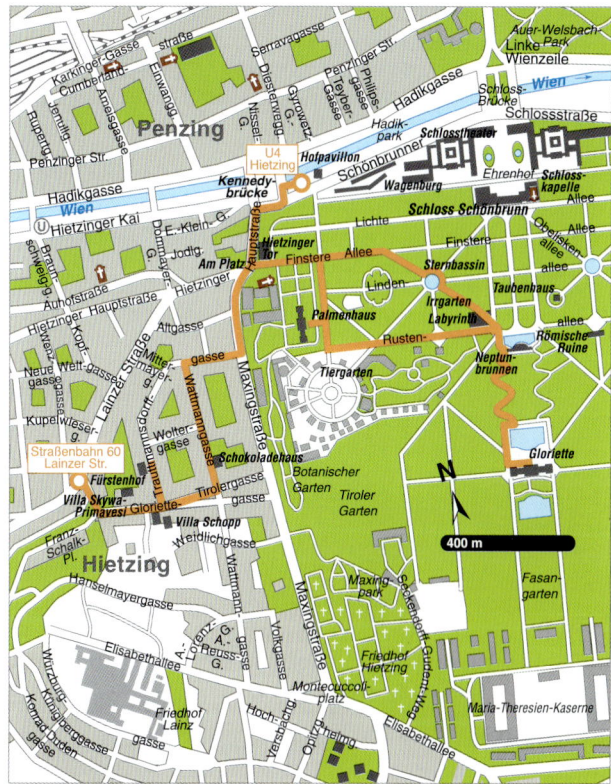

SCHÖNBRUNN-HIETZING

Enjoy the varied pleasures of a stroll around the Schönbrunn palace gardens before exploring the nearby elegant residences of Hietzing's bourgeoisie.

Start: U4 Hietzing   **Finish:** 60 (Lainzer Strasse to U4 Hietzing)
Time: about 90 minutes

PSYCHOANALYSIS

Upsetting the World's Apple Cart

Critics of Sigmund Freud's theories and practice of psychoanalysis often complain that what they consider his excessive emphasis on people's sexual inhibitions derives from the fact that he was working in Vienna in 1900. The patients who provided the raw materials for his scientific observations were mainly women, members of the emotionally uptight—or as Sigmund himself would put it, sexually repressed—Viennese bourgeoisie.

Freud's supporters would argue that just because Viennese society presented ideal conditions for the revelation of his uncomfortable ideas did not make them less valid. The conservative establishment of the Austro-Hungarian Empire was resisting new, potentially subversive ideas of any kind, in politics, art or science. Coming on top of revolutionary socialism, the erotic painting of Gustav Klimt and Egon Schiele and the 12-tone music of Arnold Schoenberg, here was this fellow talking about child sexuality, seduction theory, the Oedipus complex, penis envy and the death drive.

Not nice. But if psychoanalysis is justly defined as a method of studying the mind and treating mental and emotional disorders based on revealing and investigating the role of the unconscious mind, it's always going to be uncomfortable.

Cure or Disease?

Born of a Jewish family in 1856 in Moravia (now part of the Czech Republic), the troublemaker grew up in Vienna where he received a medical degree in 1881. Five years later, an announcement appeared in the Viennese press: "Dr Sigmund Freud, Lecturer in Neuropathology at the University of Vienna, has returned from a six-month stay in Paris and now resides at Rathausgasse 7." There he opened his first practice, moving in 1891 to larger premises at what was to become one of the world's most famous addresses, Berggasse 19, near the University.

Those six months in Paris had been spent with Dr Jean Martin Charcot studying nervous diseases, in particular hysteria. Back in Vienna, Freud collaborated with Josef Breuer on the theory that symptoms of hysterical patients could be traced directly to psychic trauma in earlier life. At first, they tried hypnosis to reveal these trauma, but Freud soon found it more effective to get patients to delve into their unconscious by a process of free association of ideas, drawing notably on matter retrieved from their dreams. He extended the process beyond hysteria to other mental and emotional disorders. Publication of his *Interpretation of Dreams (Traumdeutung)* in 1900 and *Psychopathology of Everyday Life (Zur Psychopathologie des Alltagslebens)* in 1901—analysing what became known as "Freudian slips" in speech, forgetfulness and other mistakes in everyday behaviour—won him worldwide acclaim.

The reception in Vienna was considerably less positive. The powerful Catholic establishment and prim and proper bourgeoisie led the attack on Freudian psychoanalysis for licensing extravagantly uninhibited erotic self-expression in cabaret, cinema, theatre and painting. Lumping Freud's theories with Marxism, philosopher Karl Popper said "All these systems try to explain too much." Leading social critic Karl Kraus noted in his satirical magazine *Die Fackel* (The Torch) that in the city's coffeehouses like the Grienstiedl, self-centred intellectuals had not waited for Freud to expound their theories about secret nervous states and the condition of the soul for solving the mysteries of life. To be fair—not one of Kraus's preoccupations—Freud himself had always envied the psychological insights of playwright and novelist Arthur Schnitzler, his "secret knowledge" of the human heart. Kraus delivered his guillotine-like conclusion: "Psychoanalysis is the disease whose cure it claims to be."

Freud was well aware of the ravages threatened by his revolutionary ideas, what he himself called "the plague" he was bringing to America on a trip in 1909. But the most devastating Viennese reaction was the resistance of his professional peers, most often the thundering silence and indifference. While doctors in Zurich, Berlin, Budapest, London and New York reacted with enthusiasm, fellow members in the Vienna Society of Physicians dismissed his ideas as "unbelievable" or "nonsense". A professor at the Society for Psychiatry and Neurology pointed out that since hysteria came from the Greek word for "uterus", it was idiotic for Freud to suggest that a man could be hysterical.

Disciples and Adversaries

From 1902, Freud formed the Wednesday Psychological Society *(Psychologische Mittwochsvereinigung)* named after his weekly Wednesday meetings with disciples in the waiting room at Berggasse 19. It became the more formal Vienna Psychoanalytical Society before moving in 1910 to the College of Physicians. Among early adherents was Alfred Adler (1870–1937), but the master rejected this ardent socialist's insistence on concepts such as the inferiority complex being conditioned as much by social forces as by the patient's individual unconscious. Adler went on to form his own school of Individual Psychology, focussing particularly on children with theories that have continued support both in Europe and the United States.

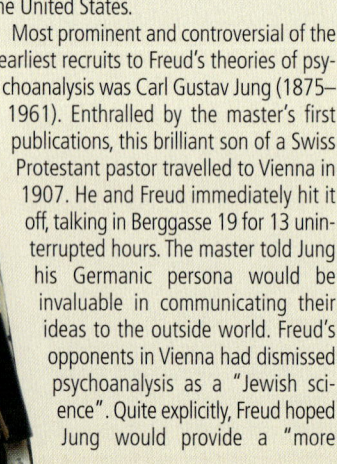

Most prominent and controversial of the earliest recruits to Freud's theories of psychoanalysis was Carl Gustav Jung (1875–1961). Enthralled by the master's first publications, this brilliant son of a Swiss Protestant pastor travelled to Vienna in 1907. He and Freud immediately hit it off, talking in Berggasse 19 for 13 uninterrupted hours. The master told Jung his Germanic persona would be invaluable in communicating their ideas to the outside world. Freud's opponents in Vienna had dismissed psychoanalysis as a "Jewish science". Quite explicitly, Freud hoped Jung would provide a "more respectable" gentile façade. But by 1912 they had parted company over Jung's commitment to mysticism, the occult and both Christian and pagan mythology from which he developed his concepts of "psychic totality", "energism", archetypes and a universal collective unconscious. Jung found Freudian concepts excessively centred on sexuality, most notably the Oedipus complex observing a child's attraction toward the parent of the opposite sex and its rivalry and outright hostility toward the parent of its own sex.

So Why Vienna?

Irony has always been a stock-in-trade of Viennese life. Freud himself was not unaware of the supreme irony of presenting such uncomfortable ideas as a son's incestuous feelings towards his mother to a city that has always valued above all else its psychological comfort and all-round *Gemütlichkeit*. It was a town with which he entertained throughout his life a relationship of love and hate. The ambivalence that Vienna inspires in many of its citizens was perhaps essential for a scientific discipline that swept away clear-cut certainties about our behaviour.

Freud could not bring himself to leave until June 1938, three months after the Viennese had cheered the German Army marching in along Mariahilfer Strasse. He died the next year, exiled in London, but his ideas have continued to influence our thinking, Many have been contested for some of their outdated sexism, but most often for the abusive charlatanism practised by irresponsible distorters of his methods. However, whether we like them or not, we are stuck with his revelations of the impact of the unconscious on our everyday behaviour.

Further reading:
Sigmund Freud: *An Outline of Psychoanalysis* (1940)
Irvin D. Yalom: *When Nietzsche Wept: a Novel of Obsession* (1992).

EXCURSIONS

We propose here four day trips from Vienna, revealing more delights of the countryside away from the pomp and splendour of the capital. The first is close to the city and can be reached by subway or tram.

THE ENVIRONS AT A GLANCE

SIGHTS

Architecture
Heiligenstadt 74
Eisenstadt 77

Monasteries
Klosterneuburg★ 75

Heiligenkreuz............75
Melk★ 76

Romance
Mayerling.................76

Atmosphere
Nussdorf 74
Grinzing★ 75

Baden 76
Neusiedler See★ 77

WALKING TOUR 78

WINING AND DINING 89

KAHLENBERG

This walk takes you through the villages of Heiligenstadt, Nussdorf and Grinzing at the foot of Kahlenberg slope. If you have the time, the hike to the top is rewarded with a grand panoramic view.

Heiligenstadt When you arrive in Heiligenstadt, take a look at the impressive Karl-Marx-Hof, a pioneering housing estate that stretches over 1 km and has more than 1,600 apartments. It was built at the end of the 1920s by Karl Ehn, an important architect of Vienna's Social Democrat era, but still seems startlingly modern in appearance. Begin your walk in the footsteps of Beethoven, who lived at Probusgasse 6. In this house, now set out as a small museum, the composer wrote his *Heiligenstädter Testament*, a letter to his brother in which he describes his increasing deafness and feeling of isolation. 🆄 4: Heiligenstadt

Nussdorf Perched high over the Danube, the village boasts several nicely located Heuriger wine gardens. Operetta composer Franz Lehar owned a country mansion here, which is now open to the public. Kahlenbergstrasse meanders up to the vineyards. The walk involves a little effort, but it is repaid with a stunning view over the Danube and Alps from the terrace of a restaurant at the top of the hill. You may also like to visit the Josefskirche with its pictures of the Turkish siege of 1683. Ⓢ **40 to Nussdorf**

Grinzing A side trip on the way to the Kahlenberg goes to this pretty village, famous for its Heuriger wine gardens. Cobenzlgasse and Höhenstrasse offer an easy path up the Kahlenberg. Wander a while around the village to seek out its attractive houses and old wine presses. There's also an elegant late-Gothic church with a copper dome. It is worth driving on to the Leopoldsberg as the view from there is splendid. This hill is named after Leopold III of Babenberg, founder of Klosterneuburg Abbey. Ⓤ **4: Heiligenstadt then Bus 38A**

WIENERWALD
The Vienna Woods offer splendid opportunities for exploring the hinterland. The scenery in these last foothills of the Alps is very romantic, perfect for long walks beneath the pine trees, their needles crackling underfoot.

Klosterneuburg Leopold III of Babenberg founded this abbey (Stift) in the 12th century on the spot where, according to popular legend, his hunting dogs found the lost veil of his wife Agnes. Austria's first major Romanesque monastery was partially destroyed at the beginning of the 18th century. Karl VI had it rebuilt as a combination of palace and church. The imposing imperial staircase (Kaiserstiege) leads to the living quarters. Gothic and baroque paintings and sculptures are displayed in a museum. Leave some time free to visit the frequently reconstructed basilica, St-Leopold-Kapelle, in which you can see the tomb of Leopold III, sanctified in the 15th century. • **Daily 9am–6pm. Guided tours in English Sat, Sun and holidays at 2pm** • **12 km (7.5 miles) from Vienna.** Ⓢ **or Bus 238, 239**

Heiligenkreuz This Cistercian monastery was founded by Burgundian monks on behalf of Leopold III of Babenberg in 1135. It was named for what is believed to be a piece of the True Cross, brought back from the Holy Land by Leopold himself and now kept in the monastery. Visit the Gothic and Romanesque church, monastery and chapter-house. • **34 km (20 miles) southwest of Vienna** • **Autobahn A21** • **Bus 265 from Südtirolerplatz**

Mayerling This peaceful little market town became known thanks to the tragic event which shook the empire at the end of the 19th century. Crown Prince Archduke Rudolf shared the liberal ideas of his mother, Empress Elisabeth. He supported the demands of the Hungarian parliamentary opposition and set a large part of the Austro-Hungarian aristocracy against him. He fell in love with the 17-year-old Baroness Maria von Vetsera and asked for his marriage with Stephanie of Belgium to be annulled by the pope. Rudolf's father Franz Joseph was against it and demanded an end to the adulterous love affair. On January 30, 1889, Rudolf killed his mistress in his hunting lodge and then committed suicide. Franz Joseph had a Carmelite convent built on the site of the lodge.
• **36 km (22.5 miles) southwest of Vienna • Autobahn A21**

Baden The site of this charming town was already known in Roman times for its hot sulphur springs. In the 19th century the imperial court came regularly to take the waters at the elegant spa resort. Beethoven lived at Rathausgasse 10. You can use the thermal baths or try your luck at the casino. • **26 km (16 miles) south of Vienna • Autobahn A2 Ⓢ from the Staatsoper**

THE WACHAU
Less than 100 km (60 miles) west of Vienna is the countryside of the Danube Valley. Castles and monasteries were built on rocky spurs high above the river.

Melk The hilltop monastery of Melk towers majestically over the town. It was the seat of the Babenberg family from the 10th century onwards. Leopold III handed the castle over to the Benedictines who built it into a fortified monastery. At the end of the 18th century it was rebuilt in baroque style by Abbot Dietmayr. With its symmetrical towers and central dome, the church dominates the ensemble of monastery buildings. • **100 km (60 miles) west of Vienna • Autobahn A1**

BURGENLAND
This is Austria's easternmost province, bordering Hungary. It boasts Europe's largest steppe lake, the Neusiedler See, and is also renowned for its wines. The provincial capital is Eisenstadt. Relatively flat, it is great for hikers and cyclists.

EXCURSIONS 77

Vineyards surround the charming village of Grinzing.

Neusiedler See The lake is part of the Neusiedlersee-Seewinkel National Park. The reserve covers some 14,000 ha (34,600 acres) of Austrian and Hungarian territory and is blessed with abundant flora and fauna. The lake is shallow and ringed by a belt of reeds in which more than 300 species of birds live and breed. On the east shore, make a stop at Rust, protected as a national monument with its picturesque houses. In July and August, the townsfolk live in huts built on stilts.In Mörbisch, 3 km (2 miles) from Rust, the dazzling white houses evoke the villages of nearby Hungary. A road through the water-reeds leads to a bathing area. From mid-July to the end of August, this enchanting region hosts an operetta festival. • **60 km (37 miles) southeast of Vienna • Autobahn A4**

Eisenstadt Visit the former palace and winter residence of the Esterhazy family, in particular the ceremonial hall where Haydn wrote most of his masterpieces. In summer you can sit out at one of the terrace cafés. • **Southeast of Vienna • Autobahn A3**

WALKING TOUR: HEILIGENSTADT-GRINZING

From the Fernsprechamt bus stop on Grinzinger Strasse, turn right on Nestelbachgasse to Pfarrplatz. Built over an ancient Roman settlement, the Romanesque **St. Jakobskirche** stands beside one of Beethoven's three Heiligenstadt homes, a 17th-century house (Pfarrplatz 2) where he lived in 1817. Leave the square along Probusgasse to the **Beethovenhaus** (No.6) in which the composer wrote his despairing Heiligenstadt Testament in 1802. It is now a museum with a charming inner courtyard and garden of fruit-trees at the rear. At the end of Probusgasse, turn left on Armbrustergasse past the **Bruno Kreisky Forum**, an international think-tank named after the Austrian Chancellor.

A right turn on Grinzinger Strasse leads past one of Vienna's oldest Heuriger wine-gardens at No.66, **Weinbau Wanderer** (1606) where you can peek into the cellar storing its Nussberger wines both in ancient casks and modern stainless steel vats. In 1808, Beethoven lodged in the house next door (64) with university student Grillparzer and the future poet's mother.

From Grinzinger Strasse, fork right on tree-shaded Sandgasse past elegant villas to walk around Grinzing's picturesque wine-taverns on Himmelstrasse and Cobenzlgasse, one of the best being the 300-year-old **Heuriger Reinprecht** with its yellow and white façade at Cobenzlgasse 22. The chimes of the Baroque belfry, riding above the otherwise late Gothic **Pfarrkirche zum Heiligenkreuz,** call its parishioners to drink the good wine in moderation. For an unkitschy Heuriger away from the crowds, go south on Grinzinger Allee (or take the 38 tram to Paradisgasse station) and turn left on Iglaseegasse to the pretty **Hengl-Hasenbrunner** wine-garden at No.10.

EXCURSIONS

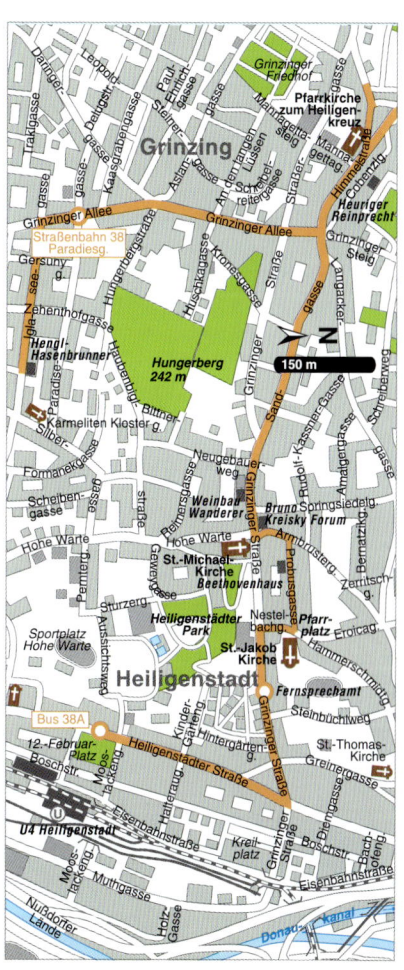

OUT IN THE COUNTRY

Beethoven soothed his nerves by moving out to Heiligenstadt. Enjoy its rural tranquillity before tackling the merry bustle of Grinzing's Heuriger taverns.

Start: U4 Heiligenstadt Bus 38A

Finish: 38 (Grinzing)

Time: about 50 minutes

A TASTE OF VIENNA

Exploring the cuisine of Vienna is to make a journey around the Austro-Hungarian Empire. Many of the choicest Bohemian, Hungarian, Serbian and North Italian delicacies ended up in some form or another in the kitchens of the capital's best hotels and restaurants and became "Viennese". Nowhere is the imperial origin of a culinary dish more evident than in the *Wiener Schnitzel*. This breaded veal cutlet may have made its first appearance in Vienna as early as the 14th century, but according to legend, it was not until 1857 that it became the revered dish it remains to this day. That was the year that Field Marshal Josef Graf Radetzky, commanding officer of the Austrian armies in the North Italian territories of Lombardy and the Veneto, brought the recipe for *costoletta alla milanese* back to Vienna. This trophy, received as triumphantly as any banner from a defeated army, is served as a fillet much thinner than the Milanese version and with lemon, capers and potato salad rather than pasta. It became known only in 1900 as *Wiener Schnitzel* and today, you may often find it served as pork *(vom Schwein)*. But for purists and Habsburgian nostalgics, only veal *(vom Kalb)* will do. A "down-market" but delicious version of the *Wiener Schnitzel* is the *Backhendl*, chicken prepared in the same way.

Totally at home in Vienna, *gulasch* is a savoury nod to the Hungarian part of the empire—a thick stew of beef, veal or pork, in the better restaurants sometimes all three, with garlic, onions, paprika, tomatoes and celery. Also from Hungary, the spicy *Debreziner* sausages are a regular feature on the menus of popular *Beisl* (bistrots), as are sweet Palatschinken pancakes.

Bohemia (Czech Republic) is famous for its dumplings—*Knödel* in Vienna, where they have become a staple in soups and to sop up the sauces in main course dishes such as roast goose (from Polish Galicia). They also make a splendid dessert surprise with a piping hot apricot in the middle, *Marillenknödel*, or damson plum, *Zwetschgenknödel*.

Most imperial of all is a simple soldier's dish, the favourite of Austria's beloved simple soldier, Emperor Franz-Joseph himself—*Tafelspitz*. Dress it up how you will, *Tafelspitz* still boils down to boiled beef and green vegetables. Admittedly, at its best, it is the tenderest piece of beef from the rump, the *Schwanzstück*, the piece closest to the tail. It can be spiced up with *Kren* horseradish sauce. Diehard monarchists toast the Emperor with the first bite.

Apple Strudel

1 kg of cooking apples, peeled and finely sliced
200 g ready-made strudel pastry
150 g fresh breadcrumbs (even better if you fry them in butter first)
100 g sugar
50 g melted butter
50 g raisins
50 g finely chopped almonds or hazelnuts (optional)
a good pinch of powdered cinnamon
juice and grated peel of 1 lemon
20 ml rum
icing sugar

Lay out a sheet of pastry on top of a rectangle of baking paper and "paint" it with melted butter. Place another sheet of pastry on top of the first, paint with butter, repeat till all the pastry is used up. Sprinkle the top layer with breadcrumbs. Mix the apples with nuts, raisins, sugar, cinnamon, rum, lemon juice and grated lemon peel; spread the drained mixture over the pastry, leaving a border of 3 cm on each side. Fold the left and right edges over the filling then, beginning with the longest side, use the baking paper to roll up the strudel. Pinch the ends together to seal. With the help of the paper, transfer the strudel delicately to a baking sheet. Brush with the remaining melted butter, then bake for 45–55 minutes at 180–200°C till golden-brown. Before serving, sprinkle with icing sugar.

cityBites

The city's equivalent of the French bistrot, the Beisl is a cosy and relatively inexpensive meeting place to sample unpretentious Viennese specialities, wine and beer. We have also included a selection of fine restaurants, as well as some good coffeehouses, a Viennese institution that's a cross between a café and a restaurant, a place where you can while away the day reading newspapers, observing other people, playing chess, gossiping, or eating cakes and pastries.

The Heuriger is another local institution, taking its name from the new white wine. The growers are permitted to sell a certain amount directly to the public. Take a trip to the outskirts of town to sip a glass or two in the fresh air and eat a simple meal. You will frequently be entertained by typical Viennese songs, to the accompaniment of violin, guitar and accordeon. The season runs from March to October.

The three price categories are as follows (excluding drinks)

1️⃣ under €25 2️⃣ €25–50 3️⃣ over €50

CITY CENTRE

Brezl'Gwölb
1st, Ledererhof 9
☎ 533 88 11
Daily 11.30am–1am
Food served to 11.30pm
Book ahead.
[2]
Charming restaurant in a pretty setting; in summer you can sit outside. Traditional Viennese cuisine. Classical music.

Café Alt Wien
1st, Bäckerstrasse 9
☎ 512 52 22
Sun–Thurs 10am–2am,
Fri, Sat to 4am
[1]
A dark and cosy place, popular with night owls. The gulasch is good, and so is the chocolate cake.

Bräunerhof
1st, Stallburggasse 2
☎ 512 38 93
Mon–Fri 8am–9pm;
Sat 8am–7pm; Sun and holidays 10am–7pm
Live music Sat, Sun and holidays 3–6pm
[1]
Popular with writers, formerly the favourite haunt of Thomas Bernhard.

Café Central
1st, Herrengasse 14
(Palais Ferstel)
☎ 533 37 64 24
Mon–Sat 7.30am–10pm;
Sun and holidays 10am–10pm
[1]
At the end of the 19th century, the town's most famous literary café counted Stefan Zweig and Leon Trotzky among its clients. It is set in the former stables of the Palais Ferstel. A statue of writer Peter Altenberg sits in one corner near the entrance. Piano music every evening 5–10pm.

Café Griensteidl
1st, Michaelerplatz 2
☎ 535 26 92
Daily 8am–11.30pm
[1]
Another legendary literary café. Dignified, subdued atmosphere. Garden.

Café Hawelka
1st, Dorotheergasse 6
☎ 512 82 30
Mon, Wed–Sat 8am–2am; Sun and holidays 10am–2am
[1]
Founded by the Hawelkas in 1936, this café was popular with the local avant-garde set in the 1960s. The interior has remained unchanged to the present day. It gets crowded after 10pm when delicious fresh Buchtel are served (yeast buns with plum jam filling).

Café Sacher
Hotel Sacher
1st, Philharmonikerstrasse 4
☎ 514 560
Daily 8am–midnight
[1]
This is the place to indulge in a large slice of the original luscious Sacher-Torte; you can also try the famous chocolate liqueur with a hint of apricot. You may have to queue to get in.

Demel
1st, Kohlmarkt 14
☎ 535 17 17-0
Daily 10am–7pm
[1]
The window display of this famous pastry shop is simply glorious, the cake selection irresistible. Try to get a table in the front room, with its mirrors and splendid décor; you feel as though you're sitting in your own chocolate box. You can watch the confectioners at work through a window.

Do & Co
1st, Stephansplatz 12
☎ 535 39 69
Haas-Haus, 7th floor
Daily noon–3pm and 6pm–midnight
[1]
International and Viennese cuisine. This is an elegant restaurant

Griechenbeisl

with the bonus of a unique view over the Stephansdom.

Drei Husaren
1st, Weihburggasse 4
☎ 512 10 92 0
Daily noon–3pm and 6pm–1am Hot dishes served till 11pm
3

Traditional Viennese cuisine for gourmets. Reservation advised.

Figlmüller
1st, Wollzeile 5
☎ 512 61 77
Daily 11am–10.30pm
Closed in August
1

Connoisseurs recommend the enormous Wiener Schnitzel. Another branch at Bäckerstrasse 6 (daily noon–midnight, closed July, ☎ 512 17 60).

Griechenbeisl
1st, Fleischmarkt 11
☎ 533 19 77
Daily 11.30am–1am; service 11.30am–11.30pm
1

Vienna's oldest inn dates back to the 15th century. It's very popular with tourists but is worth a visit for the décor and traditional cuisine.

Gulaschmuseum
1st, Schulerstrasse 20
☎ 512 10 17
Mon–Fri 9am–midnight; Sat, Sun from 10am
1

Near the Stephansdom: 15 kinds of goulasch, even a chocolate one.

Kleines Café
1st, Franziskanerplatz 3
Mon–Sat 10am–2am; Sun, holidays 1pm–2am
1

Small café, great charm, with interior design by Hermann Czech. Pleasant terrace in summer overlooking the peaceful square.

Oswald & Kalb
1st, Bäckerstrasse 14
☎ 512 13 71
Daily 6pm–2am (hot dishes served till 1am)
2

VIENNESE SPECIALITIES

There's no escaping the *Wiener Schnitzel*: a thin slice of veal, dipped in egg and breadcrumbs and quickly sautéed. *Tafelspitz* consists of lean boiled beef, vegetables and sautéed potatoes, served with apple and horseradish sauce. For a change, how about a hearty goulash with dumplings (*Knödeln*)? Desserts also deserve a mention: a slice of chocolate cake served with a generous helping of whipped cream (*Schlagobers*), pancakes filled with cream or jam (*Palatschinken*) or *Apfelstrudel* (or any other kind of strudel for that matter—like *Mohnstrudel* with poppy seeds, *Topfenstrudel* with white cheese).

SACHERTORTE

Franz Sacher created this rich chocolate cake for a gala dinner in honour of Chancellor Metternich in 1832. Traditionally it has a filling of a thin layer of apricot jam and is often served with whipped cream. It can be ordered from Hotel Sacher, Philharmonikerstrasse 4, from the online shop, www.sacher.com or by telephone, 514 560; they send it all over the world securely packed in wooden boxes. Other cafés—for example, at the Hotel Imperial and Demel (www.demel.at; ☎ 535 17170)—make their own claims to superiority. Eduard, the son of Franz Sacher, was an apprentice at Demel, official suppliers to the emperors and kings, and perfected the recipe there. A story is told of an absent-minded American who left his papers in the famous hotel, forgetting both its name and its address. He sent a telegram to "Hotel Chocolate Cake, Vienna". It was duly delivered to Sacher.

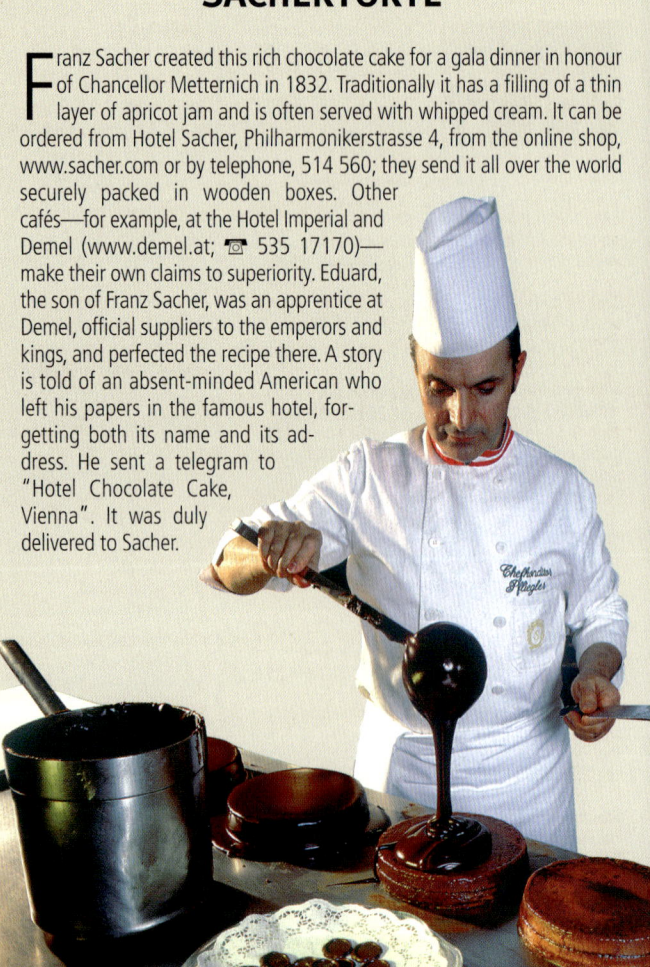

Palmenhaus

Excellent cuisine; this is one of most popular Beisln in the city so it's worth booking.

Palmenhaus im Burggarten
1st, Burggarten (Albertina entrance)
☎ 533 10 33
Mar–Oct daily 10am–2am (exact hours on www.palmenhaus.at)
2

Beautiful café-restaurant-brasserie-bar in the Jugendstil greenhouse of the Hofburg palace gardens. Sometimes live music.

Plachutta
1st, Wollzeile 38
☎ 512 15 77
Daily 11.30am–midnight
Booking ahead
Terrace
2

The Plachutta restaurants owe their fame to their Tafelspitz (boiled beef). Elegant ambience, pleasant service. Also in the 16th district, Hietzing and Nussdorf.

Steirereck
1st, Am Heumarkt 2A
☎ 713 31 68
Mon–Fri 11.30am–2.30pm and from 6.30pm
Book ahead
3

Excellent restaurant, offering exceedingly good value for money. Delicious food, friendly service, fine wine cellar.
Another branch: Meierei im Stadtpark (p. 88)

Tempel
2st, Praterstrasse 56
☎ 214 01 79
Tues–Sat 6pm–midnight (inner courtyard)
Book ahead
2

Simple, pleasant setting for ambitious and intricate cuisine, excellent wine list. The menu changes weekly; vegan and vegetarian dishes can be provided on request. Good value for money.

Vincent
2nd, Grosse Pfarrgasse 7
☎ 214 15 16
Mon–Sat 5.30pm–midnight
3

Cosy atmosphere, intriguing menus and good wine list. Vegetarian meals can be ordered in advance. Big non-smoking area.

THE HOFBURG

Café Hofburg
1st, Innerer Burghof
☎ 241 00 0
Daily 10am–6pm
1

Attractive coffeehouse with terrace in the inner courtyard of the Hofburg. Hot dishes such as goulasch and Kaiserschmarrn, a kind of sweet fluffy omelette, and snacks.

THE RING

Café Landtmann
1st, Dr-K.-Lueger-Ring 4
☎ 24 100-0
Daily 7.30am–midnight (service 11.30am–11.30pm, breakfast to 3pm)
Spacious terrace in summer.
1

Near the Burgtheater, opposite City Hall. Nice and cosy, this bourgeois coffeehouse was a haunt of Sigmund Freud.

Café Österreicher im MAK
1st, Stubenring 3–5
☎ 714 01 21
Daily 8.30am–1am, hot dishes served up to 11.30pm
2

Café-restaurant of the Museum für angewandte

Kunst (Applied Arts). Handsomely painted ceiling. International and Viennese cuisine, served in summer on a pleasant terrace in the inner courtyard.

Café Prückel
1st, Stubenring 24
Daily 8.30am–10pm
Live piano music Mon, Wed 7–10pm; terrace in summer
[1]
1950s setting. The cakes are home-made, the choice of newspapers is abundant and the waiters in their formal dress are first class and discreet. Summer terrace.

Café Schwarzenberg
1st, Kärntner Ring 17
☎ 512 89 98
Sun–Fri 7am– midnight; Sat 9am–midnight.
[1]
The first café on the Ring. Cakes, strudel and snacks. Live music Thurs, Fri 7.30–11pm, Sat, Sun 5–8pm (piano and violin).

Café Stein
9th, Kolingasse 1
☎ 319 72 41
Mon–Sat 7am–1am,
Sun from 9am
[1]
Catch up with your e-mails in this trendy cyber-café near the Votivkirche.

Glacis Beisl

Poetry readings, short film presentations, and so on. Perfect for Sunday brunch. Summer terrace.

das möbel
6th, Burggasse 10
☎ 524 94 97
Daily 10am–1am
[1]
Not only can you eat and drink in this trendy café, you can also buy the furniture, all by young designers.

Glacis Beisl
MuseumsQuartier
Entrance Breitgasse 4
7th, Museumsplatz 1
☎ 526 56 60
Daily 11am–2am
[1]
Attractive venue in the MuseumsQuartier with a large garden shaded by walnut trees. Classical Viennese cuisine.

Meierei im Stadtpark
3rd, Stadtpark
☎ 713 31 68
Mon–Fri 8pm–11pm
Sat, Sun 9am–7pm
[2]

A restaurant serving six-course meals plus appetizers, a cheese bar set in the ageing rooms where you can sample up to 150 varieties, and the stylish ess.bar for snacks (Mon–Fri from 5pm).

Neu Wien
1st, Bäckerstrasse 5
☎ 512 09 99
Mon–Sat 6pm–1am
(book after 22.30pm)
[2]
Fashionable restaurant decorated with paintings by popular Vienna artist Christian Ludwig Attersee.

Niky's Kuchlmasterei
3t, Obere Weiss-gerberstrasse 6
☎ 712 90 00
Mon–Sat non-stop noon–midnight
Book ahead
[3]
Fine wine cellar, original décor. To sample house specialities request the Degustationsmenü.

Wiener Rathauskeller
1st, Rathausplatz 1
☎ 405 12 10
Mon–Sat 11.30am–3pm and 6–11.30pm
[2]
In the basement of the City Hall, several restaurants with different price ranges and a wine bar (Tues–Sat 5–10pm).

KARLSPLATZ AND BELVEDERE

Café Museum
1st, Operngasse 7
☎ 586 52 02
Mon–Sat 8am–midnight;
Sun and holidays
10am–midnight
1

Alfred Loos's revolutionary décor was destroyed in World War II. Rebuilt to the original plans in 2003.

Weidinger
4th, Danhausergasse 3
☎ 505 56 97
Mon–Fri 11am–11pm
1

Inviting inn with peaceful shady garden. Wiener Schnitzel and other local specialities.

OUTER DISTRICTS

Café Gloriette
Schönnbrun Park
☎ 879 13 11
Daily 9am–park closing time
1

Lovely view over the palace and gardens; excellent food. Musical breakfast Sun 9.30–11.30am

Café Sperl
6th, Gumpendorferstr 11
☎ 586 41 58
Mon–Sat 7am–11pm
Sun 11am–8pm
Closed Sun in July and August
1

Popular with billiard- and card-players. Home-made cakes, friendly service.

Fuhrgassl-Huber
Neustift am Walde 68
19th, Döbling
☎ 440 14 05
Bus 35A : Neustift am Walde
Mon–Sat 2pm–midnight;
Sun and holidays
noon–midnight
1

In winter, enjoy the comfort of this elegant restaurant tastefully furnished in wood. Self-service at hot and cold buffet.

Sirbu
Kahlenberger Str. 210
19th, Döbling
☎ 320 59 28
Bus 38A to terminus, then 15 minutes' walk
Mon–Sat 3pm–midnight
Closed mid-October to early April
1

One of the town's best Heuriger. The wine is very good.

Welser
Probusgasse 12
19th, Döbling
☎ 318 97 97
Bus 38A: Fernsprechamt
Daily 3.30pm–midnight
1

Copious buffet, home-made strudels. Music.

Weltcafé
9th, Schwarzspanierstr. 15
☎ 405 37 41
Daily 9am–2am
1

All food and drinks are made from organic and fair-trade produce.

Wolff
Neustift am Walde
19th, Rathstrasse 50
☎ 440 37 27
Daily 11am–1am
1

Traditional vineyard inn with a rich and varied buffet, rustic decor and sheltered courtyard.

EXCURSIONS

Bach-Hengl
Sandgasse 7–9
19th, Grinzing
☎ 320 24 39
🚋 38
Daily 4pm–midnight
1

Typical atmosphere. Wine has been produced here since the 12th century.

Bach-Hengel

CityNights

As a capital of good living, Vienna offers plenty of opportunities for entertainment. To forget the rigours of winter, the Viennese brighten up their evenings with concerts, operas, theatre plays and intoxicating balls. In fact, for the Viennese, concert-going is part of their daily routine. They will often dash straight from work to the concert hal, ever eager to hear for the umpteenth time a performance of Mozart's 41st Symphony. Afterwards, they will avidly discuss the way the conductor interpreted the music and led the orchestra, and make a date for the next event. The season lasts from September to June.

Wien-Programm, the monthly listing of events, is available at all tourist information offices and ticket offices. Many theatres sell tickets on Internet; you can also call in at:
Wien-Ticket
Linke Wienzeile 6
Daily 9am–8pm
☎ 588 85
www.wien-ticket.at

THEATRE TICKETS

Agencies charge a commission in the region of 20% for seat reservation. However, you can book your tickets directly at the theatre or concert hall, or online. It's best to make your reservations at least three weeks in advance. For the Akademietheater, Burgtheater, Staatsoper and Volksoper, all belonging to the Federal Theatre Association (*Bundestheaterverband*), there are commission-free sales offices at Bundestheater-Holding GmbH, Goethegasse 1. Telephone orders (payable by credit card) on 514 44 78 80, Mon–Fri 8am–6pm; Sat, Sun 9am–noon.

Prater
🅄 1: Praterstern
🚅 O, 5, 21: Praterstern
☎ 728 95 16
Volksprater (amusements) mid March to end October, daily 10am–1am; free entry to the site, open 24h a day
Giant ferris wheel (Riesenrad) May–Sept daily 9am–1am; Nov–Feb 10am–8pm; March, Apr, Oct 10am–10pm
This huge park, covering some 1,300 ha (526 acres), was the emperor's hunting ground in the 16th century. Joseph II opened it up to the public in 1766 and the Prater became an amusement park for young and old, with everything from roller-coaster to ghost train. The giant ferris wheel erected for the World Exhibition of 1897 with its famous red cabins dominates the whole park and offers a magnificent view of the city from a height of 65 m (213 ft). The wheel was destroyed in World War II and restored in 1947. It achieved world fame in Carol Reed's film *The Third Man*. On the Praterhauptallee are also the Planetarium and the Lusthaus, a former hunting lodge. The Restaurant Schweizerhaus is worth a visit for its famous *Stelzen* (veal or pork shin).

THEATRE

Akademietheater E6
🅄 4: Stadtpark
3rd, Lisztstrasse 1
☎ 514 44 47 40
Excellent repertoire of classical and contemporary plays.

Burgtheater C3
🅄 3: Minoritenplatz or
🚅 1, 2, D: Burgtheater
1st, Dr-Karl-Lueger-Ring
☎ 514 44 41 40
The Burgtheater built in 1888 in Italian Renaissance style is considered the best theatre in the German-speaking world, and it's claimed that the purest and best German is spoken here. The programme ranges from European and German classics to the parodies of 19th-century Viennese playwright Johann Nestroy.

Dschungel Wien-Theaterhaus für junges Publikum C5
🅄 2: MuseumsQuartier

In the MuseumsQuartier, 7th, Museumsplatz 1
☎ 522 07 20-20
An art and culture centre for children and young people aged 2 to 22. Drama, dance, workshops, music and so on.

Schauspielhaus C1
🚋 D: Bauernfeldplatz
9th, Porzellangasse 19
☎ 317 01 01-18
Ticket office weekdays 4–6pm, and from 6pm before performances
The theatre founded in the 1970s for underground works today puts on plays by modern Austrian and foreign writers.

Theater in der Josefstadt B3
🚋 J: Theater in der Josefstadt
8th, Josefstädter Str. 26
☎ 427 00-300
The great director-producer Max Reinhardt worked in this theatre from 1920 to 1930. It opened in 1788. The productions are often more popular in appeal than those of the Burgtheater and make a pleasant contrast with the classical décor. The Kammerspiele (1st, Rotenturmstr. 20, ☎ 427 00-300) is also part of the Josefstadt Theatre.

Volkstheater C1
Ⓤ 2, 3: Volkstheater
Neustiftgasse 1
☎ 521 11 400
☎ 521 11-131 (evening)
This old theatre stages modern, avant-garde productions and operettas, but Shakespeare, too.

MUSIC

Musikverein E6
Ⓤ 1, 2, 4: Karlsplatz
🚋 1, D, J: Kärntner Ring
🚌 2, 62, 65: Opernring
1st, Bösendorferstr. 12
☎ 505 81 90
Ticket sales begin one month before concert date. Information: ☎ 505 81 90. Telephone sales by credit card only. Ticket sales at the concert hall: Mon–Fri 9am–8pm; Sat 9am–1pm.
Open September 1–June 29
The New Year's Day concert broadcast all over the world begins on January 1 at 11am in the grand Goldener Saal, which is renowned for its outstanding acoustics. It seats 2,000. Ticket sales for the following New Year's concert begin on January 2. The Brahmssaal is used for chamber music recitals, with the Vienna Philharmonic holding 18 concerts each year.

Raimund-Theater (off map by A7)
Ⓤ 3, 6: Westbahnhof
6th, Wallgasse 18–20
☎ 599 77-0
Operettas and musicals.

Ronacher E5
Ⓤ 1, 3: Stephansplatz
Ⓤ 4: Stadtpark
1st, Seilerstatte 9
☎ 514 11-0
Recently re-opened after extensive renovation. It mainly shows Broadway hits translated into German.

Staatsoper D5
Ⓤ 1, 2, 4: Karlsplatz
🚋 1, 2, D or J: Oper
1st, Opernring 1
☎ 514 44 22 50
Programme information: Telephone sales by credit card only: 513 15 13 daily 10am–9pm
Tickets are put on sale one month before the performance (see also p. 92). Remaining seats are sold at the opera house on the day of performance, from 10am until one hour before the curtain rises. The best standing-ticket tickets are sold 80 minutes before the start of the performance. The Vienna Opera is the last opera house in the world with a permanent repertoire of some 150 works.

LET'S GO OUT TONIGHT

The Viennese are known for their fondness for etiquette and chivalry—Austria cultivates its traditions, and older gentlemen may still graciously kiss a lady's hand when introduced. If you want to be accepted, they should be respected. Dress decorously for opera, theatre and concerts. If you are attending a great ball like the Opera Ball, then white tie and tails for the gentleman and long evening dress for the lady are a must. Costume-hire (rental) shops can help you out if necessary.

Theater an der Wien D6
U 1, 2, 4: Karlsplatz
6th, Linke Wienzeile 6
☎ 588 85
Ticket office daily 10am–7pm

Playwright and actor Emanuel Schikaneder founded this theatre in 1801. The première of Mozart's *Magic Flute*, for which he had written the libretto, was performed ten years earlier on the same site near the entrance to the Naschmarkt, as was Beethoven's *Fidelio* in 1805. In 2006 the theatre was the main venue for concerts celebrating the 250th birthday of Mozart.

Volksoper off map by C1
U 6: Volksoper
🚋 40, 41, 42: Volksoper
9th, Währingerstrasse 78
☎ 514 44 36 70
Telephone sales by credit card only: ☎ 513 15 13

The "People's Opera", built in 1898 for the 50th anniversary of Franz Joseph's coronation, is devoted to operettas, and the occasional opera. Productions are first-rate but less classical than at the Staatsoper.

Wiener Konzerthaus E–F6
U 4: Stadtpark
3rd, Lothringer Str. 20
☎ 242 002
Telephone sales by credit card only.
Sale at the theatre
Mon–Fri 9am–7.45pm;
Sat to 1pm

This handsome Jugendstil building was erected in 1912 by the Vienna Concert Society. Symphonic music is performed in the Great Hall (Grosser Saal), chamber music in the Mozart and Schubert halls. All the concerts featuring world-famous soloists are outstanding in quality.

Wiener Sängerknaben
Augartenpalais
☎ 216 39 42
Office: Mon–Thurs 9am–5pm; Fri to 3pm
Mass in Hofburgkappelle (entrance on Schweizerhof) Sun 9.15am (except July and Aug). Advance booking essential

The Wiener Sängerknaben boys' choir was founded in 1498 under Emperor Maximilian I. Their

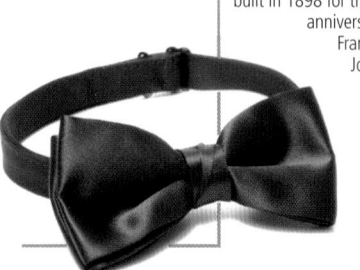

concerts were once reserved for select audiences. Joseph Haydn and Franz Schubert were both members of the choir. The angel-voiced boys still wear sailor suits for performances.

BARS

Barfly's Clu
U 3: Zieglergasse
Hotel Fürst Metternich
6th, Esterhazygasse 33
☎ 586 08 25
Daily 6pm–3am
Popular bar with an infinite choice of whiskies and rum.

Blue Tomato
U 3: Johnstrasse
15th, Wurmsergasse 21
☎ 985 59 60
May–Sept Mon–Thurs 7pm–1.30am; Fri, Sat to 3am
Cellar and garden in inner courtyard, mainly jazz.

First Floor
U 1, 4: Schwedenplatz
1st, Seitenstettengasse/Rabensteig
☎ 533 78 66
Mon–Fri 5pm–3am
Sat, Sun 7pm–3am
Cocktail bar with a huge aquarium.

Halbestadt
U 6: Währinger Strasse
9th, Währinger Gürtel, Stadtbahnbogen 155
☎ 319 47 35
Sun–Thurs 7pm–2am, Fri–Sat to 4am
A cocktail bar in a tramway arch designed by Otto Wagner.

KIX Bar
U 1, 3: Stephansplatz
1st, Bäckerstrasse 4
☎ 0676 603 82 29
Mon–Fri 6pm–2am; Sat 8pm–2am
High walls in garish colours, minimalist furniture, reminiscent of New York style. Very good cocktails.

Krah Krah
U 1, 4: Schwedenplatz
1st, Rabensteig 8
☎ 533 81 93
Daily 11am–2am; hot meals served to 1.30am
Good selection of beers, tasty sandwiches. Casual atmosphere.

Loos American Bar
U 1, 3: Stephansplatz
1st, Kärntner Strasse 10
☎ 512 32 83
Thurs–Sat noon–5am, Sun–Wed noon–4am
Tiny bar designed by Adolf Loos in 1908, a Jugendstil gem.

Miles Smiles
U 2: Volkstheater
8th, Lange Gasse 51
☎ 405 95 17
Sun–Thurs 8pm–2am; Fri, Sat 8pm–4am
Concerts for jazz fans.

Onyx-Bar
U 1, 3: Stephansplatz
1st, Stephansplatz 12
Haas-Haus, 6th floor
☎ 535 39 69-492
Mon–Sat 9am–2am
Cocktail bar, view of Stephansdom.

Shultz
✈ 49 or Bus 13A Kirchengasse
7th, Siebensterngasse 31
☎ 522 91 20
Mon–Thurs 9am–2am; Fri, Sat 9am–3am; Sun 5pm–2am
This popular Sixties bar is bright and pleasant.

Sky Bar
U 1, 4: Karlsplatz
1st, Kärntner Strasse 19
Steffl 7th floor
☎ 513 17 12
Mon–Sat 1pm–3am; Sun 6pm–2am
Fashionable bar with an infinite list of cocktails; magnificent view over Stephansdom and the city centre.

WRITING IN VIENNA

Austria's capital has a literature and theatre that are as distinctively Viennese as its cuisine—but a lot spicier. To begin with, the German spoken in Austria is not the same as that of Germany, and the difference becomes most apparent in Vienna. Even in the hands of its literary giants, the language has a recognizable "nonchalance", offering a subtle blend of casual "street" usage and formal elegance that German writers just don't allow themselves.

Anti-Heroics of the 19th Century
If the classical drama and exuberant lyrical poetry of Franz Grillparzer represented a consciously patriotic Austrian response to the 19th-century German literary heroics of Goethe and Schiller, the seductive nonchalance of Viennese writing soon became apparent in the popular comedies of Johann Nepomuk Nestroy and Ferdinand Raimund.

Born into a prominent Viennese bourgeois family, Nestroy brought a rough, tough realism in sarcastic reaction against the solemn tragedy and sentimentality of traditional theatre. He peppered the unashamedly superficial plots of his farces with improvised satirical songs which managed to enrage both liberals and conservatives, leading up to the revolutionary age of 1848. Typically, *Der böse Geist Lumpazivagabundus* depicts a struggle between the forces of love and money, an eternal Viennese theme.

Ferdinand Raimund similarly explored the romantic and cynical contradictions of human nature. He began as an apprentice pastry-cook selling delicacies at the illustrious Burgtheater and went on to create bittersweet comedies with a mixture of melancholy and farce, highlighted by eccentric costumes and extravagant décor.

"Young Vienna"
The modern era of Viennese literature came into its own at the turn of the 20th century. In his literary magazine, *Moderne Dichtung*, critic Hermann Bahr formulated the whole idea of modernity with an essay anticipating the "death of the exhausted world" *(Tod der erschöpften Welt)* represented by the moribund Habsburg Empire. The creation of what came to be known as the Wiener Moderne ("Vienna Modern") coincided with the heyday of the

city's coffeehouses. A lively bunch of writers gathered at the Café Griensteidl, later at the Café Central: Peter Altenberg, Alfred Polgar, Felix Salten and Egon Friedell, working as poets, short-story writers and *Feuilletonisten* (essayists) for the literary magazines and newspapers' arts pages, but also playwrights Arthur Schnitzler and Hugo von Hofmannsthal. The literati were loosely grouped under the title *Jung-Wien*, "Young Vienna", many of them contributing to what was also a golden age of satirical cabaret.

Arthur Schnitzler (1862–1931) was drawn in his plays, novels and, particularly, his short stories *(Leutnant Gustl and Fräulein Else)* to the psychology of his characters. On his 50th birthday, Sigmund Freud saluted the medically trained Schnitzler as a "colleague" in his investigation of the "underestimated and much-maligned erotic". In his *Reigen* (Hands Around) and *Liebelei* (The Reckoning), he broke with the stifling inhibitions of his own bourgeois milieu, and with Professor Bernhardi he met head-on the prevalent stench of anti-Semitism in Vienna's "polite" society.

With hindsight, the town has been delighted to identify with Peter Altenberg's declaration: "Art is art and life is life, but to live life artistically: that is the art of life." This could also have been coined as an aesthetic creed for Hugo von Hofmannsthal (1874–1929). This son of a patrician banker brought a heightened hedonism to his poetry and theatre. His aesthetic preoccupation is apparent in the *Elektra* he rewrote for

Richard Strauss's opera (1909), and again in his libretti for Strauss's *Der Rosenkavalier* (1911) and *Ariadne auf Naxos* (1912).

Observing all this with an excoriating wit, Karl Kraus (1874–1936) was the era's outstanding but also in many way most unpleasant social critic, by way of his magazine, *Die Fackel* (The Torch), founded in 1898 and for which he was from 1911 the only contributor. First and foremost, Kraus championed a new honesty and precision for the German language, determined to rid it of superfluous aesthetic pretensions. He railed against what he saw as the Austrian capital's boundless corruption, hypocrisy, superficiality and decadent sensuality, typified for him by Franz Lehar's hugely popular operetta *Die lustige Witwe* (The Merry Widow). Though elsewhere often startlingly misogynous and, despite being born of Jewish family, vehemently anti-Semitic, Kraus is justly honoured for his brilliant (if unperformable) satirical drama of World War I, *Die letzten Tage der Menschheit* (The Last Days of Humanity).

After the Ball Was Over

In the aftermath of World War I, the Habsburg dynasty crumbled and Viennese literature took stock. Reporter and novelist Joseph Roth (1894–1939), as a Jew born in the Austro-Hungarian Empire's Polish Galicia, saw that multi-cultural empire as the only state which enabled him to be both "a patriot and citizen of the world". Consequently, after years of radical left-wing journalism, Roth's best-known novel, *Radetzkymarsch* (1932), looks back on the Habsburg era with wistful nostalgia.

Robert Musil (1880–1942) was less charitable. Regarded along with the masterpieces of Marcel Proust, Thomas Mann and James Joyce as one of the 20th century's greatest novels, Musil's long, but unfinished *Der Mann ohne Eigenschaften* (The Man Without Qualities) is a merciless depiction, among other things philosophical and psychological, of the fatuity and decay of Viennese society.

Stefan Zweig (1881–1942) held himself as a man apart, above the fray of Vienna's 20th-century landscape. Though passionately anti-war, he remained in his fiction and historical biographies the genteel, urbane cosmopolitan, relentlessly unpolitical in a world screaming out for commitment. Fellow writers criticized Zweig for making no public denunciation of Nazism when his famous name might have helped the anti-fascist cause. Driven into exile, he wrote his autobiographical *Die Welt von Gestern* (The World of Yesterday), despairing that there was no place left for him. He went on to commit suicide in Brazil. His best-known work is *Schachnovelle* (The Royal Game).

Since 1945, Thomas Bernhard (1931–89) and Elfriede Jelinek, the two outstanding figures of Vienna letters, have both been attacked by the Viennese themselves as *Nestbeschmutzer*—people who dirty their own nest. Both have been severely criticized for focusing on the Austrians' failure to confront their complicity in the crimes of Hitler's Third Reich. Bernhard's play *Heldenplatz* (Heroes' Square) was given its premiere in 1988, to celebrate the Burgtheater's centenary, but also exactly 50 years after Adolf Hitler addressed cheering crowds on the Heldenplatz in front of Vienna's Hofburg, the play's recurring theme.

Novelist Elfriede Jelinek, who won the Nobel Prize for Literature in 2004, has been similarly controversial in such politically committed works as *Die Kinder der Toten* (The Children of the Dead). As a feminist, she also dealt with sexuality, aggression and abuse in personal relations. Writing in Vienna remains an uncomfortable business.

More Viennese writers worth reading:
Ingeborg Bachmann (1926–1973): *Malina*, a novel; *Darkness Spoken*, collected poems
Ilse Aichinger (1921–): *Herod's Children; The Bound Man and other stories*
Adalbert Stifter (1805–1868): *Colourful Stones*
Friederike Mayröcker (1924–): *Morbus Kitahara*
Christoph Ransmayr (1954–): *The Last World*

cityFacts

Airport	102
Bicycles	102
Climate	102
Driving	102
Emergencies	102
Entry Formalities	103
Fiaker Cabs	103
Handicapped Visitors	103
Lost Property	103
Money	103
Museums	103
Post Office	104
Public Holidays	104
Safety	104
Shopping	105
Taxis	105
Telephone	105
Tipping	106
Toilets	106
Tourist Information Offices	106
Tours	107
Trains	107
Transport	107

Airport

Vienna-Schwechat international airport lies about 20 km (12.5 miles) southeast of the city centre. There is a tourist information office (7am–10pm) and bureau de change (6am–8.30pm, as well as the major car rental companies. The City Airport Train (CAT) shuttles every 30 min between the airport and Wien-Mitte (16 minutes to the City Air Terminal); €8 single, €15 return. The buses of the Vienna Airport Lines go to the South and West railway stations, with good connections for the U-Bahn, and the express Schnellbahn S2 to Wien-Mitte (travel time approx. 25 minutes). Information ☎ +43 1 7007 222 33 www.viennaairport.com

Bicycles

Cycle lanes are common in the city centre. For €2 per day you can hire a bike with the Citybike Tourist Card, obtainable from Royal Tours, Herrengasse 1–3, 1st district, daily 9–11.30am and 1–6pm, ☎ 710 46 06. The first hour is free.

Climate

Vienna has a continental climate. Winters can be harsh and snowy, with temperatures in January and February down to –15°C (–9°F); in summer the thermometer may climb to 35°C (95°F).

Driving

Driving on the motorway requires a special permit which can be bought for one or two weeks or for a whole year. The speed limit on the motorway is 130 kph (80 mph), on country highways 100 kph (60 mph) and in town 50 kph (30 mph). Seat-belts are compulsory. Children under 12 must sit in the back in special safety seats.

Parking in town is permitted only in designated zones. Regulatory parking permits *(Parkschein)* can be purchased in tobacco shops (Trafik), the post office or in railway stations.

Emergencies

In Austria as in the rest of the EU, the general emergency number is 112.
Police: 133   Fire: 122   Ambulance: 144

Entry Formalities
Austria is a member of the European Union (EU) and signatory of the Schengen Agreement. If you are a citizen of an EU country, you should nonetheless take a valid passport or identity card. Travellers from non-EU countries may import, duty-free, 200 cigarettes, 100 cigarillos, 50 cigars or 250 g tobacco, 1 litre of spirits or 2 litres of wine.

Fiaker Cabs
These open coaches drawn by two horses have been trotting through the streets of Vienna for over 300 years. Fiaker ranks are stationed at several major tourist locations, notably Michaelerplatz and Stephansplatz. Agree on the price before setting out. A short tour, lasting 15 to 20 minutes, costs 40 Euro, a longer one (34–40 minutes) 65 Euro, an hour 95 Euro.

Handicapped Visitors
Tourist information offices distribute a brochure Vienna for Handicapped Visitors *(Wien für Gäste mit Handicaps)*. Enquire beforehand by telephone to see if a monument or museum offers wheelchair-access. Public transport is not easily accessible to disabled people, as most buses and trams have steps. The subway (U-Bahn) is better equipped.

Lost Property
The lost property office, Fundamt, is at Bastiengasse 36–38, open Mon–Wed and Fri 8am–3.30pm. Thurs to 5.30pm; ☎ 01 40 00 80 91

Money
The currency is the Euro, divided into 100 cents. Coins: 1, 2, 5, 10, 20 and 50 cents, 1 and 2 euros; banknotes: 5, 10, 20, 50, 100, 200 and 500 euros.

The city centre has plenty of automatic cash-distributors. Most restaurants and hotels accept credit cards.

Banks and currency exchange offices open Mon–Fri 8am–3pm (Thurs to 3.30pm). Small offices close 12.30–1.30pm

Museums
To check on opening hours, consult www.wien.gv.at

Post office

The main post office, Fleischmarkt 19, is open daily 6am–10pm. Other branches open Mon–Fri 8am–noon and 2pm–6pm

Public Holidays

Jan 1	Neujahrstag	New Year
Jan 6	Heilige Drei Könige	Twelfth Night
May 1	Tag der Arbeit	Labour Day
Aug 15	Mariä Himmelfahrt	Assumption
Oct 26	Nationalfeiertag	National Holiday
Nov 1	Allerheiligen	All Saints' Day
Dec 8	Mariä Empfängnis	Immaculate Conception
Dec 25	Weihnachten	Christmas Day
Dec 26	Stefanitag	St Stephen's Day

Movable holidays:

Easter Monday	Ostermontag
Ascension Day	Auffahrt
Whit Monday	Pfingstmontag
Corpus Christi	Fronleichnam

Fasching (Carnival) begins on November 11 at 11.11am and lasts until Ash Wednesday; the Ball season "proper" begins with the Kaiserball (Emperor's Ball) December 31.

The music season begins in September. Ask at tourist information offices for detailed programmes.

In December, Christmas trees are set up in Schönbrunn park and in front of City Hall, and there's a traditional Christmas market, Christkindlmarkt, on City Hall square.

Safety

By and large, Vienna is a safe place. Nonetheless, as in all big cities, take sensible precautions against pickpockets. Do not flaunt your valuables carelessly in crowded places. If you lose your passport or identity cards, contact your embassy or consulate (see addresses below).

Shopping

Popular gifts from Vienna range from craftware, embroidery and porcelain to confectionery and wines. There are also typical traditional waistcoats or embroidered Dirndl peasant skirts, and all kinds of kitsch. The most exclusive shops are on and around the Graben (Meinl am Graben, a top-class delicatessen and wine store with upstairs restaurant at no. 19), Kohlmarkt (designer boutiques, and Demel at no. 14), and Kärntner Strasse (Österreichische Werkstätten crafts at no. 6, Petit Point for meticulously embroidered items at no. 16, Kaufhaus Steffl, a big department store, at no. 19 and Lobmeyr glassware at no. 26). There's an elegant shopping mall, the Ringstrassen-Galerien, at Kärntner Ring 5–7. Mariahilfer Strasse in the 7th district is a bustling shopping street with several department stores and international trend-setting boutiques. It's said that Beethoven did his shopping at Zum Schwarzen Kameel on Bognergasse 5, not far from the Graben. One of Vienna's oldest shops, it sells gourmet delicacies and wines.

In the numerous antique shops in and around the Dorotheergasse you will find paintings, rococo and Biedermeier (19th-century) grandfather clocks and furniture, memorabilia of the Habsburgs and countless portraits of Franz Joseph and Sissi. At no. 17 is the Dorotheum, an internationally renowned auction house. On the ground floor, for people not in the mood to bid, are items sold at set prices. The Musikhaus Doblinger at no. 10 sells musical scores, books and magazines.

Shops usually open Mon–Fri 9am–6.30pm, Sat 9am–6pm. Supermarkets often stay open on Thursdays to 9pm, and many shopping streets have one night late opening, for example Mariahilfer Strasse Thursday to 9pm.

Taxis

They can be hailed on the street or ordered by phone on 31 300, 40 100, 60 160 or 81 400. Rates are higher at night from 11pm to 6am, and on Sundays and public holidays. An alternative, in the city, is the original, rapid and environmentally friendly bicycle-taxi (Faxi): ☎ 0699 120 05 624.

Telephone

Telephone cabins take coins or phone-cards—available at tobacco shops (Trafik)—and a few accept international credit cards.

Rates are cheaper between 8pm and 8am and from Friday 6pm to Monday 8am
Information: ☎ 11 88 99
For other countries (Europe and elsewhere): ☎ 11 82 00

Tipping
Over and above the official service charge most often included in the bill, it is customary to leave a tip of 5–10% in hotels, restaurants and cafés.

Toilets
Public toilets are generally open 9am–7pm. Some restaurant or coffee-house facilities also require a small tip to the attendant.

Tourist Information Offices
For brochures and other information before you leave home:
  Wien Hotels & Info
  Wien-Tourismus
  A-1025 Wien
  ☎ +43 1 211 14-0
  Fax + 43 1 24 555-666
  e-mal: info@wien.info
  www.wien.info

For information on the spot, hotel bookings, maps, currency exchange and city tours:
  Tourist-Info
  Albertinaplatz (corner of Maysedergasse)
  Daily 9am–7pm
  Phone and fax numbers, and postal address as above.

For up-to-date information about what's on in Vienna, see the website:
  www.viennahype.at

Tours

For tours on specific themes, such as Jugendstil architecture or design, enquire at Tourist- Info Wien.

River cruises, from May to October:
DDSG Blue Danube,
☎ 588 80
www.dsg-blue-danube.at

Trains

Timetable information is available on www.oebb.at or by telephone, 143 (0)5 1717. This applies to trains for West- and Südbahnhof, Wien Mitte, Wien Nord and Franz-Josephsbahnhof.

Transport

The Vienna subway (U-Bahn) and tramway operate efficiently. The subway is open from 5.30am to midnight. Comprehensive information is available at the Karlsplatz subway office. At street level, station are indicated by signs with a white U on a blue background.

Note that the tramlines are being reorganized, especially along the Ring. From 26 October 2008 the old lines N and 65 become **Line 1**: Prater Hauptallee – Schwedenplatz – Ring – Opera – Stefan-Fadinger-Platz (for the Hundertwasser-Haus and the Prater). Lines J and N become **Line 2**: Ottakringer Strasse – Opera – Ring – Schwedenplatz – Friedrich-Engels-Platz (from the Parlament past the Opera and MAK to Urania). In the course of 2009, Line D will become Line 3, and line 71 will be incorporated into Line 4.

The Wien-Karte is a cut-rate ticket permitting unlimited travel on subway, tram and bus for 72 hours. The same ticket gives you discounts at many museums, shops and restaurants, shows and guided tours, on 4 days. It can be purchased in hotels, the tourist office on Albertinaplatz, public transport sales offices or online at ww.wienkarte.at. 2008 price: €18.50

Day tickets, 3-day and 7-day tickets are also available. These must be punched in a machine the first time they are used.

Children under 6 travel free; under-15s pay half price and travel free on Sun, public holidays and school holidays. Information: www.wienerlinien.at

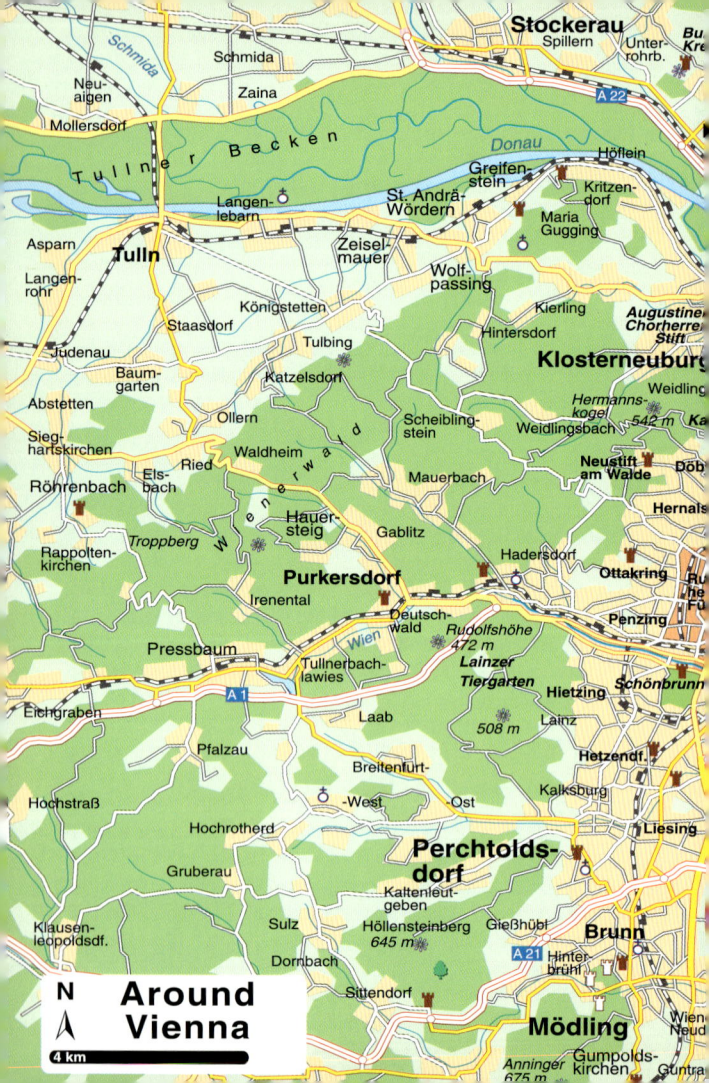

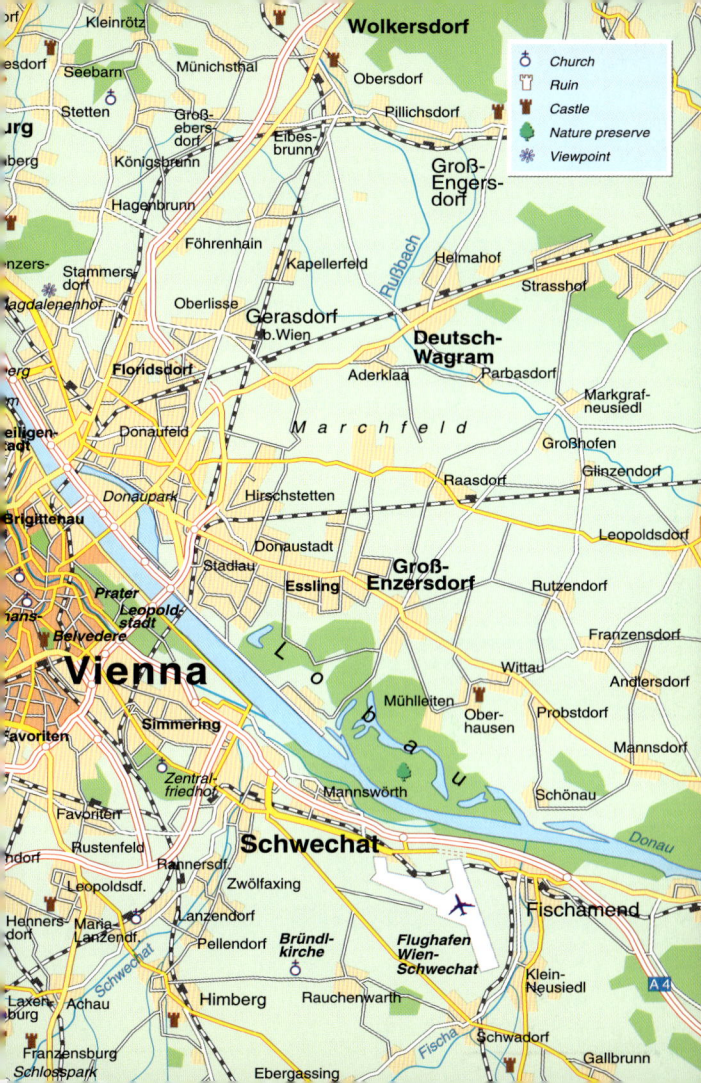

INDEX

Akademie der bildenden Künste 54
Akademietheater 92
Albertina 39
Altes Rathaus 34
Am Hof 28
Amerlinghaus 40
Annagasse 32
Apfelstrudel 81
Augustinerkirche 39
BA–CA Kunstforum 27
Bäckerstrasse 30–31
Baden 76
Barockmuseum 54
Beethovenhaus 78
Beethoven Pasqualatihaus 42–43
Belvedere 54–55
Böhmische Hofkanzlei 34
Börse 34
Bruno Kreisky Forum 78
Bundeskanzleramt 26
Burgenland 76–77
Burgtheater 40, 43–44, 92
Christkindlmarkt 59
Café Central 27, 84
Coffee 30
Coffeehouses 84–89
Danube Canal 48
Danube cruises 59
Demel 25, 84
Donauinsel 59
Dr-Karl-Lueger Church 62
Dschungel Wien Theaterhaus für junges Publikum 92–93
Eisenstadt 77
Ethnology Museum 38
Feuerwehrmuseum 28
Fleischmarkt 31
Franziskanerplatz 31
Freyung 27
Fuchs-Villa 62
Graben 24–25

Grinzing 75
Haas-Haus 24
Haus der Musik 32–33
Haus des Meeres 59
Heiligenkreuz 75, 78
Heiligenkreuzer Hof 34
Heiligenstadt 74, 78
Herrengasse 26–27
Hietzing 68
Hofburg 36–39, 58
Hohe Brücke 34
Hoher Markt 30, 34
Holocaust Memorial 29
Hotel Imperial 53
Hundertwasser, Friedensreich 62
Jesuitenkirche 34
Judenplatz 29
Jüdisches Museum 26
Kahlenberg 74–75
Kaiserappartements 36–37
Kaisergruft 33
Kapuzinerkirche 33
Karlskirche 53
Karlsplatz-Pavillons 53
Kärntner Strasse 32
Kirche am Steinhof 63
Klimt, Gustav 53, 55
Klosterneuburg 75
Kohlmarkt 25
Kriminalmuseum 60
Kunsthalle 46
KunstHausWien 59, 60
Kunsthistorisches Museum 45, 59
Künstlerhaus 51
Kurrentgasse 34
Kursalon 48
Leopold Museum 46
Liechtenstein Museum 61–62
Loos-Haus 26
Majolikahaus 56
Maria am Gestade 29, 34

Mariensäule 28
Mayerling 76
Medieval Art Museum 55
Melk 76
Michaelerkirche 26
Misrachi-Haus 29
Mozarthaus Vienna 31
Museum für angewandte Kunst, MAK 46–47
Museum Moderner Kunst, MUMOK 46, 58–59
MuseumsQuartier 46
Music 19
Musikverein 51, 93
Naschmarkt 56
Naturhistorisches Museum 45
Neue Hofburg 38
Neuer Markt 33
Neues Rathaus 43
Neusiedler See 77
Nussdorf 74–75
Oberes Belvedere 55
Österreichische Galerie des 19. und 20. Jahrhunderts 55
Österreichische Nationalbibliothek 38–39
Österreichisches Theatermuseum 33
Otto-Wagner Villa 62–63
Palais Collalto 28
Palais Trautson 40
Parisergasse 34
Parlament 44–45
Peterskirche 25
Postsparkasse 47, 48
Prater 92
Raimund-Theater 93
Rauhensteingasse 32
Redoutensaal 38
Ringstrasse 44

INDEX

Ronacher 93
Ruprechtskirche 29–30, 34
St-Jakobskirche 78
St-Ulrichsplatz 40
Sachertorte 86
Schatzkammer 37–38
Schauspielhaus 93
Schlosspark Schönbrunn 66–67, 68
Schönbrunn Palace 58, 63–65
Schottenstift 27–28
Schönlaterngasse 34
Schuberts Geburtshaus 62
Secession 53–54, 56
Sigmund Freud-Museum 61
Silberkammer 36
Singerstrasse 31–32
Sisi Museum 37, 58
Sissi 15
Spanish Riding School 39, 59
Spittelberg 40
Staatsoper 46, 93
Stadtpark 46
Stephansdom 22–24
Synagoge 34
Technisches Museum 59
Theater an der Wien 56, 93
Theater in der Josefstadt 93
Theatre tickets 92
Uhrenmuseum 28
Uniqa Tower 48
Universität 42
Unteres Belvedere 54
Urania 47, 48
Völkerkundemuseum 38
Volksgarten 40
Volksoper 94
Volkstheater 40, 93
Votivkirche 42
Wachau 76
Wagenburg 66
Weinbau Wanderer 78
Wiener Konzerthaus 94
Wiener Sängerknaben 62, 94
Wiener Strassenbahnmuseum 60–61
Wienerwald 75–76
Wien Museum Karlsplatz 50
Winterpalais des Prinzen Eugen 31
Winterreitschule 38
Wipplingerstrasse 29
Zentralfriedhof 62
Zoo 67
ZOOM Children's Museum 46, 58
Zu den neun Chören der Engel 28

General Editor: Barbara Ender
Research: Linda Witeck
Photo credits: Wien Tourismus/Duffy p. 4; /Fasser p. 37; /Angermayr p. 77; Koller p. 81; /MAXUM p. 90; Bildagentur Huber/Picture Finders p. 8; /Mirau pp. 18, 27, 66–67; /Fantuz p. 52; hemis.fr/Cintract p. 12; /Frumm pp. 15, 71; /Wysocki p. 20; /Suetone pp. 30, 63; /Borgese p. 82; Wiener Mozart Orchester Photo Gallery pp. 19, 43; Renata Holzbachová pp. 23, 61, 65; Matias Jolliet pp. 25, 92, 97; Österreich Werbung pp. 39, 85(bottom), 86; /Kalmar p. 72; istockphoto.com/Xyno pp. 44, 106; /Austraat p. 51; Hackl-Haslinger p. 58 ; /Sandromo p. 59; /Banks p. 94; /Kemie p. 99; Kelli Patterson p. 47; Österreichische Galerie Belvedere Wien p. 55; KunstHausWien p. 62 (Hundertwasser, *460 Hommage au Tachisme*, 1961); www.griechenbeisl.at p. 85; www.palmenhaus.at p. 87, www.glacisbeisl.at p. 88; www.bach-hengl.at p. 89; Andreas Uebelhart p. 100
Walks and Features: Jack Altman
Layout: Matias Jolliet, Luc Malherbe
Maps: Elsner & Schichor; JPM Publications: Mathieu Germay

Copyright © 2008, 2000 JPM Publications S.A., 12, ave Fraisse, 1006 Lausanne, Switzerland
information@jpmguides.com – www.jpmguides.com

All rights reserved. No part of this book may be reproduced or transmitted in any form or by any means, electronic or mechanical, including photocopying, recording or by any information storage and retrieval system without permission in writing from the publisher.

Every care has been taken to verify the information in the guide, but neither the publisher nor his client can accept responsibility for any errors that may have occurred. If you spot an inaccuracy or a serious omission, please let us know.

Printed in Switzerland – 12553.00.4235, Weber Benteli/Bienne – **Edition 2008–2009**

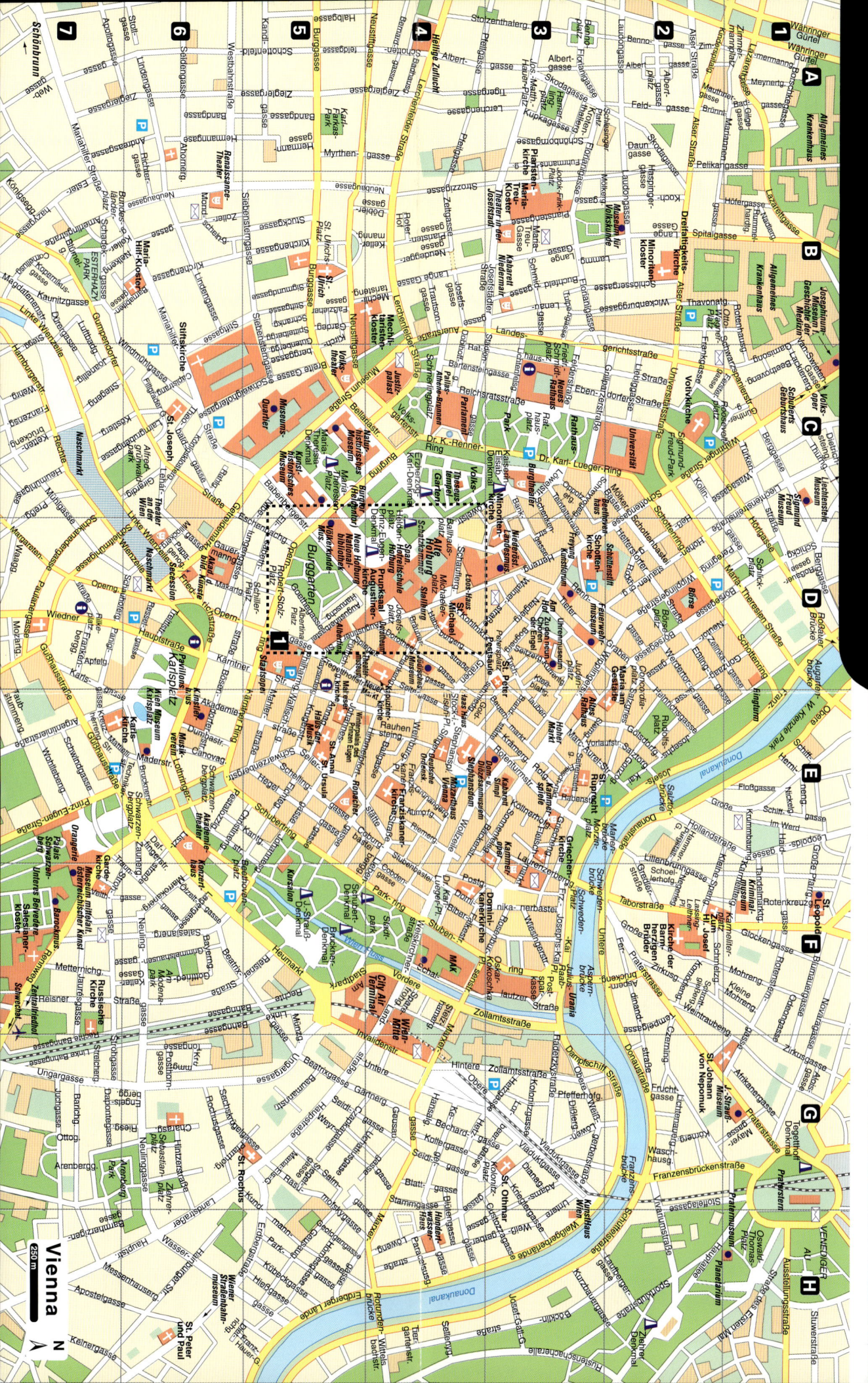

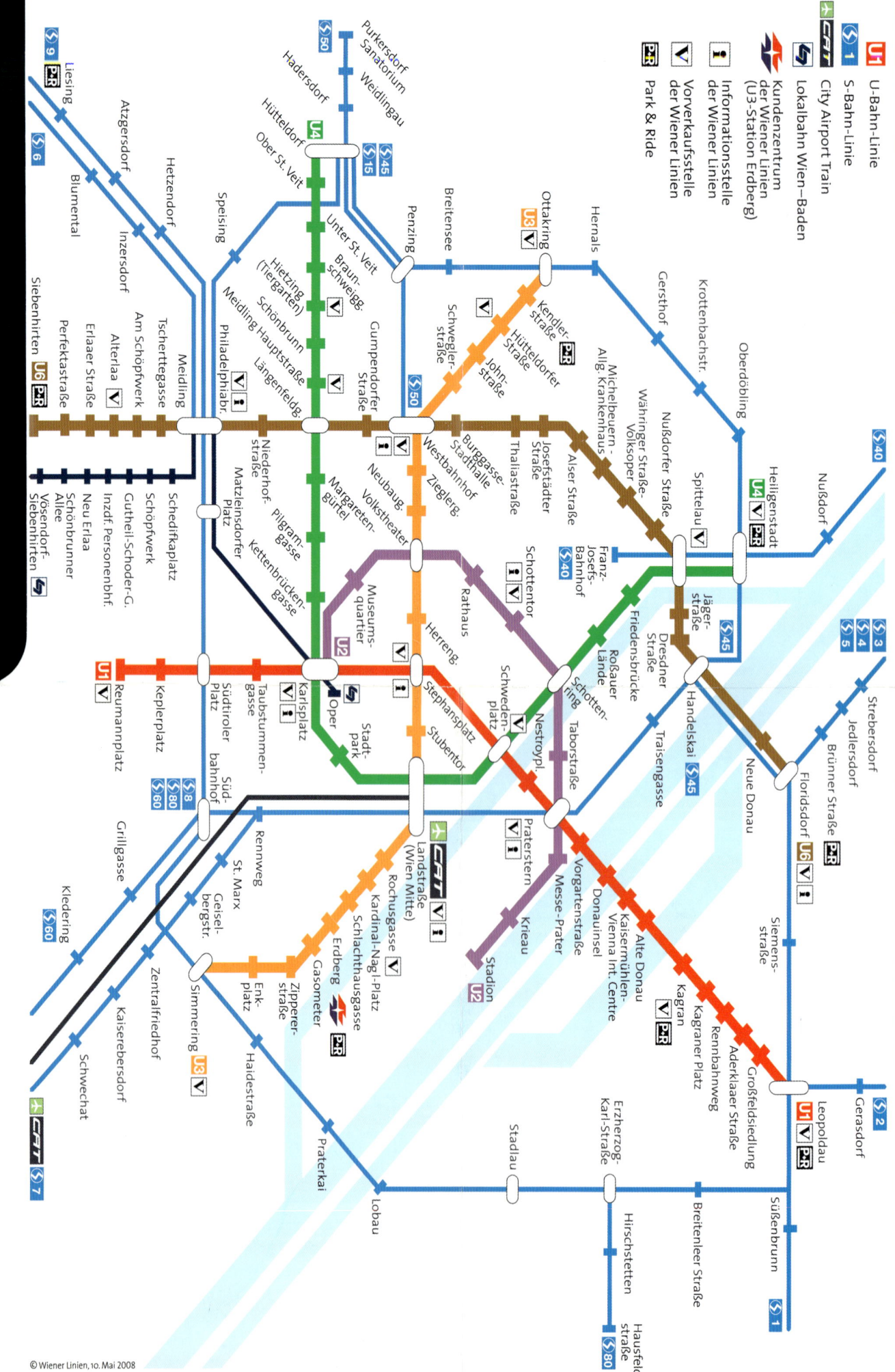